The Muffin Lady

The Muffin Lady

Muffins, Cupcakes, and Quick Breads
for the Happy Soul

Linda Fisher with Andrew Marton

ReganBooks
An Imprint of HarperCollinsPublishers

I dedicate this book to the loving memory of my mother, Catherine Sharpe Barnes

HarperCollins books may be purchased for educational, business, or sales promotional use. For information please write: Special Markets Department, HarperCollins Publishers, Inc., 10 East 53rd Street, New York, NY 10022.

FIRST EDITION

Designed by Stephanie Tevonian

Photo Credits: Photographs by Michael Lutzky appear on pages ii, 5, 6, 9, 10, 15, 18, 20, 24, 26, 36, 39, 43, 45, 48, 52, 54, 56, 59, 62, 66, 72, 86, 92, 94, 99, 103, 104, 108, 110, 122, 124, 137, 139, 141, 142, 143, 145, 147, 169, 174, 181, 191, 208, 210; photographs by John Guntner appear on pages 68, 101, 112, 151, 200; all remaining photographs are courtesy of the author's personal collection.

Library of Congress Cataloging-in-Publication Data

Fisher, Linda, 1949–
    The muffin lady : muffins, cupcakes, and quick breads for the happy soul / Linda Fisher. — 1st ed.
        p.   cm.
    Includes index.
    ISBN 0-06-039246-0
    1. Muffins. 2. Bread. 3. Cake.   I. Title.
TX770.M83F57   1997
641.8'15—dc21   97-28736

98 99 00 01 ❖/RRD 10 9 8 7 6

Contents

Acknowledgments   *vii*

Introduction   *1*

Seeds and Nuts   15

Muffins   *23*

Quick Breads   *28*

Cupcakes and Cakes   *35*

Cookies and Pastries   *36*

Fruits   39

Muffins   *49*

Quick Breads   *73*

Cupcakes and Cakes   *83*

Cookies and Pastries   *93*

Vegetables and Grains   101

Muffins   *111*

Quick Breads   *124*

Cupcakes and Cakes   *130*

Cookies and Pastries   *133*

Confections   137

Muffins   *145*

Quick Breads   *158*

Cupcakes and Cakes   *161*

Cookies and Pastries   *179*

Index   *213*

Acknowledgments

This book would not have been possible without enormous support from people too numerous to mention. Naturally, since family has always come first throughout my life, I am forever grateful to my loved ones for their unflagging support during the writing of this book.

Along my journey, from the streets of Westminster to the pages of *The Muffin Lady*, several people offered much time and help. When I was truly down and out, Ginger Hornburger pulled me up by my bootstraps. Marti O'Connell gave me my first Radio Flyer wheels to begin my journey. When times were toughest, Tony D'Eugenio was both mentor and friend. Denise Felliciano spooned out moral strength and wisdom when I needed both most. Her daughter, Melissa, has become an invaluable extension of my baking tradition. Jackie Bates came to my rescue in a moment of real need. Linda Dayton was the kind of all-around friend who never disappears when times are tough. Laurene Case invested not only money but unwavering faith in my work. The Westminster Volunteer Fire Department opened their arms and kitchen to me. Jackie Powder was the first to chronicle my story. And in this book, Andrew Marton, Jeremie Ruby-Strauss, Michael Lutzky, and John Guntner tirelessly assembled prose and picture to convey not only how I bake but who I am.

And to Jim, my most heartfelt thanks for being the faithful shepherd of my life and work.

Linda Fisher
Westminster, Maryland

Introduction

When I think of my first moments as a baker, I think back to my mother, Catherine. I can see her so clearly, as if she were still here—maybe leaning against one of the butcher-block countertops or standing next to that eggshell-white Sunbeam mixer. I remember her aprons, so typical of the 1950s. She had one that was pinafore-style with scalloped edges, and another that was nylon, with a fluffy style to it. She had one for being in the kitchen and another purely for when she greeted guests.

I also remember her music. I can't separate my mother, baking, and all kinds of music pouring from that family kitchen. My mother always had the radio on, and it tended to play the big band sounds. And when that got tiring, she switched to religious music. Naturally, she would sing along. She had a lovely voice.

While I was growing up, my week was built not on days but on what meal would be served on what day. Monday was leftovers night. Tuesday, meat loaf. Wednesday, chicken. Thursday, liver. And Friday, always fish. And then came the weekend. For me, Saturday mornings meant one thing and one thing only: my mother's pancakes. Saturdays couldn't come around fast enough for my mother to do those pancakes. Of

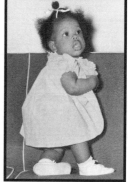

Me at a little less than one

course, I made the morning a lazy one by sleeping in, but just the thought of my mom's pancakes got me up. In fact, those pancakes were so delicious, I used to hope my mother would make them again during the middle of the week.

But that was nothing compared with Sundays, which were particularly special to all of us. The really classic southern Sunday breakfast was at my grandmother's home in Durham, North Carolina, where we would have fried chicken, rice, gravy, hominy grits, and all those buttermilk biscuits. My little old grandmother would work in front of a wood-burning stove in her white apron and long dress—all to get this meal right.

At our house, my mother took the great Sunday meal very seriously, from soup to nuts, from bread to dessert, entirely from scratch. In fact, in our kitchen, whether it was Sunday or Tuesday, there wasn't a mix in sight. I never grew up with mixes at all. It's probably why I never deal with them today. In fact, I had to marry my first husband to find out how to use a mix for anything.

Me in my stroller at just about one—I've always had a set of wheels.

Sunday was when my mother jumped to the special stuff like a standing rib roast or leg of lamb with its rosy middle, and those dinner rolls made from scratch. I loved how Mother would occasionally dye the rolls with food coloring—just for fun. I remember how we would return from Sunday church, and Mother would tie on one of those aprons and disappear into the kitchen. Soon enough, I'd hear that distinctive sound of the dough being kneaded and rolled out for those dinner rolls and wonderful pies she just loved to bake.

Sunday seemed filled with a perfume of lemon meringue, angel food, peach cobbler, and chocolate layer cakes just pouring out from the kitchen. The grand Sunday meal was truly the day when Mother would shine and we would applaud her.

Yet my mother was like a lot of women in the 1950s. They were superwomen, all wearing big "S"s on their chests. They could do it all, working Monday through Friday and taking care of the house and kids. She was pure inspiration to me. She was a career woman who, by the way, at the age of sixty-five decided to get her master's degree.

This was taken a year before my mother passed away. Check Dad out—so distinguished.

But being a homemaker was just as important to her as her career. She was still from the old school and still waited on my father—I mean to the point where she would often prepare him a separate meal, more of a soul-food, high-cholesterol meal, while she made everyone else the healthier version. Even when she was sick with cancer, she waited on my father. To the end, she remained a true southern belle.

My father, Lenzie Barnes, designed and helped build the house we grew up in. And what a house we had: a two-story structure with a slowly acquired status of showpiece. It sat high on an embankment, with antebellum columns framing the front porch. It seemed as if we had fifty zillion stairs leading up to the front door. We had a spacious kitchen, acting like a shrine to food's preeminent role in our house. The cooking area featured a butcher-block countertop, one of the first of its kind. We were particularly proud of the latest set of Formica and chrome kitchen furniture we purchased. I can still see the thick plastic padding on the chairs. Our kitchen was almost consciously segregated from the rest of the house, with a heavy swinging door as a barrier.

It would be many years, miles, and two divorces away from that comfortable Washington existence that the baking lessons I gleaned from my

My next set of wheels

family kitchen would come back to me. In 1989 I was married for a third time, was a doting mom, and had followed my nomadic husband to Rochester, New York. One day my daughter asked for a simple yellow cake with chocolate frosting. It's the kind of dessert that most young children have a craving for—at any hour of the day. I rummaged through my collection of recipes and found none that suited the request. Then it hit me like a flash of nostalgic lightning: my mother Catherine's pancake batter recipe.

What an inspiration that was. I had used that pancake recipe only for, well, pancakes. And now it hit me how easily it could be cooked in a baking pan. That was the first time I began to play with it. As if preordained, it worked the very first time I tried it.

What I didn't realize at the time was that reviving my mother's versatile recipe somehow would unlock a bushel of other concoctions, including muffins, cupcakes, and quick breads. To be sure, I had a notion of what to do with the recipe—by that time I had accumulated over twenty years of "scratch" baking experience—but I had somehow always overlooked that pancake batter, perhaps because it was so simple.

I suppose the real test of my mother's bequests to me—from that simple batter recipe to the life lessons she taught me—was in Westminster, Maryland, when my husband and I divorced in 1995. Our separation exacted quite a financial toll on me because overnight I lost the benefits of his salary.

Though I tried to keep my son and myself in our three-bedroom house, I just couldn't afford it. I received a nice loan from a friend, worth three months of living expenses, but it just wasn't enough. I had to figure out how to make ends meet.

I remembered that back when I was married and living in D.C., I had made some extra money on the side by selling baked goods, particularly my carrot cakes and muffins. So in this hour of need, I figured I would go with what I knew—baking. With the ground outside blanketed with snow, I manned my small oven and baked muffins and other goods using my mother's pancake recipe. I piled them into decorative wicker baskets and balanced them precariously on the back of a red Radio Flyer wagon. I brought my muffins door to door to such eager customers as the dry cleaner, the flower shop, a radio station, a local bank, and the city government's main office.

Quite often, on purchasing a muffin or sweet roll, people would offer a comparison

Westminster, Maryland, is warm and genuine. I love being in a town where everybody knows your name.

High-fiving Frank at the Flower Box florist shop

between one of my goods and something their grandmothers used to make. That was always the highest accolade. These grandmothers always took special care with what they did, and they seemed to do everything with such excellence. I strove to reach that same level of integrity in my own products, and the customers really appreciated it and helped me increase my business.

By October 1996, my muffin business had indeed grown, but it still wasn't enough to pay the rent. On Halloween 1996, I woke up to find myself and my son essentially evicted from our home. Up until that point I had steadfastly refused to apply for welfare. After much soul-searching, I swallowed my pride and walked across the street and asked the Carroll County Human Services office for help with housing.

By November 1996, I was set up in a rent-subsidized apartment and continued receiving child support from my son's father. It was from this small, cramped, but cozy apartment that I kept myself off welfare with my baking business. I was able to pump out as many as seven dozen muffins per day. By Christmas 1996, I was starting to pull in enough money to make ends meet, and I was actually seeing my business take shape. I thought this was my big comeback, but then in January 1997 the Health Department tried to stop me.

As I was pulling my wagon along, three of the Health Department's officers intercepted me in an alley. They were enforcing strict laws concerning selling baked goods to the public. If I didn't get a license to sell my muffins, they said, I faced a fine of up to $1,000 and ninety days in jail.

I still shake my head thinking how the Health Department officials said they really didn't want to do this to me. In the back of my mind, I was saying, "Well, then, why are you doing it?" I mean, there are crack houses and prostitutes standing on corners, and the government comes after me? What was I doing? I was pulling a wagon and trying to support my son. It wasn't as if I was driving a Mercedes or a BMW. I certainly wasn't wearing a Rolex. I didn't have furs dripping over me or a manicure and pedicure.

I was livid and breathing fire. My instinctive reaction was that I had to make people understand who I was, that I was not a doormat or stupid, and neither would I be played for a fool. I was simply trying to make a living. Pride doesn't pay the bills, but it goeth before honor. I didn't want any handouts. I wanted to work. This pride, this driving force in my life that was under attack, I got from my parents. My mother showed it in her carriage, in the way she lived. Watching her taught me not to kowtow to anyone— taught me that I was just as good as anyone else.

In what seemed like a bit of a fairy tale, everyone in the community seemed to come out to support my cause. Dozens and dozens of letters to the editor came pouring in to the local newspapers and the bigger regional ones as well. Then the Human Services office assigned to help me out told me that nearly all of the calls coming in over a several-day period had to do with my case. I think what the callers protested was the ultimate irony of my case: Here was a woman trying to stay off welfare, and another government agency was trying to prevent her from doing that—pushing her closer and closer to welfare.

I was really overwhelmed and terribly moved by all this public support for my case. People would actually stop me on the street and say how much they supported my doing my job. Others would just come up to me and say how they were behind me, that they really believed in what I was doing.

Spiritually, in this tough time, I never turned to anyone else for salvation. I did think about my late mother a lot, though. I felt her spirit in me, perhaps more than ever before. I remember so vividly being with a friend during this difficult period, and suddenly I interrupted a conversation in mid-sentence by asking her if she smelled something sweet, like vanilla? She said no. And, of course, how could she recognize that what I was smelling was my mother's scent? "Don't you smell that?" I kept asking my friend. And she didn't know what I was talking about. It was my mother's perfume that mysteriously filled the room. I think it was almost like a visitation from her.

In addition to the spiritual support I felt, there were tangible boosts as well. An anonymous donor gave me the $60 I needed for a retail food service license, so I could keep working. I was enormously grateful for this gift. I treated it as some kind of divine intervention—a blessing. And the fact that it was anonymous made me think of the notion that God has many angels, and you never really know when one will cross your path.

Also, the Westminster Volunteer Fire Department contributed to the cause in a dramatic way—by offering me, free of charge, full use of their Health Department–approved kitchen. They had expressed that they, too, were "outraged" at what had happened to me. What it all meant was that if I could manage the baking shift from 2:00 A.M. until dawn at the firehouse, I could continue my muffin business.

From that firehouse each morning I pulled my trusty Radio Flyer wagon around town, making deliveries everywhere, from the beauty parlor to—ironically—one of the satellite offices of the same Health Department that tried to shut me down. Customers lined up to pay $1.25 per muffin for the pleasure of biting into a six-ounce white chocolate or peach cobbler creation. People started to flock to my wagon, and my proportions needed to increase: Twenty pounds of flour, ten pounds of sugar, and gallons of milk for ten dozen muffins.

My growing business all seemed so natural, but I was a bit oblivious to the internal momentum it had gathered. Without intending it, I had metamorphosed into a one-woman baking conglomerate. I inherited a new name—dare I say it?—an alter ego: "the Muffin Lady."

But when all is said and done, I have been and remain a simple baker, the daughter of a professional woman and wonderful cook, and a mother myself. I saw that I had been presented

My mixer half full of rich, creamy, heavy batter

with an obstacle to overcome, and I did it. I am, in that regard, representative of a lot of people. And what unites us is that we dare to be different. With this kind of philosophy, you really can't afford to be sidetracked once you have realized what your destination is. To get there, you probably will have to question authority, just as I did. That's the one quality I have tried to instill in my children, as my parents had instilled it in me. No human being is so perfect that you need to bow down to him.

Almost losing my business reminded me that in finding my own path I have slipped into an abyss or two. And it was when the times were darkest that I realized you can rise above just about anything—especially if you are a true believer in what you're about. When you are a true believer in

In the firehouse: slicing some rolled-up buns before baking

yourself, then you can let go of the branch of security, comfort, and complacency, and move ahead. Only in letting go of that branch will you be able to take a chance. Otherwise, it is an entire life without risk. Quite frankly, you take a risk every time you pop open your eyes in the morning and again when you put that first foot out of bed. But that step has to be taken, and you must understand that sacrifices and overcoming adversity and opposition are all necessary to reach whatever goal you have set. In the end, you'll know beyond a shadow of a doubt that you've paid the dues necessary to reach your mark.

I guess you could say that my mother's recipe comes down to some basic, elemental ingredients. The spiritual ones are pride and perseverance. The material ones are sugar, flour, eggs, and milk.

My mother died in 1994. She didn't live long enough to see her simple pancake recipe reincarnated in so many forms. She also didn't live long enough to see me struggle to keep my baking business alive. But then again, she was there in a way. I consider all my baked goods from her original recipe to be a kind of tribute to her life.

I feel my mother's presence when I bake, and her recipe is the legacy I carry on.

My mom particularly loved this dress. She was such a beautiful lady.

My Mother Catherine's Pancake Batter

2 cups flour

2 tablespoons sugar

1/4 teaspoon salt

1 tablespoon baking powder

4 tablespoons butter or margarine

1/4 cup oil

2 eggs

1 1/2 cups milk

Combine all the dry ingredients. Melt the butter with the oil in the skillet used to make pancakes or in a separate small saucepan. Make a well in the center of the dry ingredients. Place the butter, oil, eggs, and milk in the well. Mix by hand (do not beat) until all the ingredients are incorporated. Spoon 1/4 cup of batter on a well-oiled hot grill. Let cook until bubbles form. Flip over and cook on the other side until golden brown.

❖ *Yield: Approximately 20 silver-dollar-size pancakes*

My Mother's Cornbread

4 tablespoons butter or margarine
¼ cup oil
2 cups cornmeal
1 cup flour
½ cup sugar

1 tablespoon baking powder
¼ teaspoon salt
2 eggs
1 cup milk

Preheat the oven to 350 degrees. Allow 10 minutes for preheating. Put the butter and oil in a 9-inch-square cake pan and place in the oven until the butter melts and browns, approximately 10–15 minutes. Combine all the dry ingredients. Make a well in the center and add the eggs and milk. Pour the melted butter and oil on top and stir gently until completely blended. Pour the batter into the same cake pan used to melt the butter. Bake for 20–30 minutes, or until light golden brown.

❖ *Yield: 8–10 servings*

My Mother's Baking Powder Biscuits

2 cups flour
2 tablespoons sugar
1 tablespoon baking powder
¼ teaspoon salt
¼ pound (1 stick) butter or
  margarine

1 egg
¼ cup milk
Paprika (optional)

Sift and combine all the dry ingredients. Cut the butter into pieces and add to the dry ingredients. Add the egg. With your hands or with the dough hook of a mixer, lightly blend or knead the dough mixture. Gradually add the milk until the mix is moist enough for both the flour and the butter to stick. It might not be necessary to use all the milk. Take the resulting mix and form by hand into a ball. Cover it with a towel or another bowl and let sit for 30 minutes.

Preheat the oven to 350 degrees. Lightly dust a board or table with flour. Roll the dough out. Cut out the biscuits with a 2-inch round cookie cutter or the rim of an 8-ounce drinking glass. Place them in a 10-inch round cake pan. It is not necessary to grease the pan. Prick each biscuit with a fork. To help the biscuits brown, sprinkle lightly with paprika if desired. Bake for 20–25 minutes, until lightly browned.

❖ *Yield: six to eight ½-ounce biscuits*

Seeds and Nuts

Call it almost a rite of passage, because I was the eldest of three daughters, and there was little doubt that I should join my mother in the kitchen and learn to cook and bake. In a way, it was all but expected of me.

My mother was always in the kitchen by herself, and I was really the only one who came in and intently watched her work. From there I would just observe her and pick things up, sort of by osmosis. I vividly remember her teaching me how to mix her basic batter by hand. Sure, we had the Sunbeam mixer in the corner, but for her pancake mix or cornbread or biscuits, it

Here I am at two with my sister Brenda.

really had to be done manually. It all made sense, considering my mother was raised during the Depression and, though hardly poverty-stricken, in the kind of household where everything was done by hand.

For my mother, the Sunbeam mixer was a luxury. In fact, my mother introduced me to the mixer for things that had nothing to do with baking, such as squeezing orange juice or whipping mashed potatoes. Later on she grew to rely on the mixer for her special cakes, especially her angel food cake—the dessert of the 1950s—and for her "seven-minute icing," that sticky marshmallow cream icing, over coconut cake.

I used to love watching my mother—was almost hypnotized by her—as she broke one egg after another into the bowl. I would just stare at the deep yellow yolks as they broke up and mixed with the sugar, causing the whole mix to turn different shades of white and yellow.

I believe in the two-handed cracking system—why mess around?

Nobody else in our family cared as much about what went on in the kitchen as I did. Besides, I think my mother felt she had to teach somebody, and I was the eldest. Looking back now, I realize that the time in the kitchen with my mom was a great bonding time for us. I was all of eleven years old, and it was in my mother's kitchen that I learned about my beautiful grandmother. A domestic for a white family in Virginia, she cooked, did laundry, and got along on three hours of sleep a night. Most of what my mother first learned about the kitchen she learned from her mother.

Sometimes we would talk about boys. It was in the kitchen that she passed on her favorite motto about men: "A man who can't do anything for you, well, you just don't need him."

There was also a practical side to my learning the ropes from my mother. As she became more and more involved in community activities, and they demanded more of her time, she needed a backup, her top helper. With all of her work outside the house, her plate was really overflowing. She was still trying to be that superwoman, being a homemaker and having a full-time job, but she couldn't do it all anymore. Later on she admitted that she had taught me to cook partially because she didn't like my father's cooking. "He kills the meat after it's already dead" is how she put it.

So when it came to cooking tips, my mother taught me simple, basic skills to handle the Monday-through-Friday meals. As for her baking secrets, she took her time unfolding them. For four years I didn't do much of anything on my own until she felt comfortable releasing me.

One of the first lessons she taught me was that I didn't need a timer to cook. All I had to have was a good nose. Your nose will tell you when it is done or nearly done. My mother never even used a timer. She just knew by smell. And I've come to realize, all these years later, that she was absolutely correct. Your nose will tell you nearly all the time when something you're baking is ready.

Cornbread was probably the first of the simple baked goods I actually could do on my own. I always associated my mother's cornbread with some kind of fish dish we had on Friday evenings. Cornbread was the quickest thing for me to learn and throw together. My mother didn't have to worry about my standing over a stove. All I had to do was make the cornbread batter, add a pinch of this and a dash of that, pour it into a pan, and shove it into the oven.

Cornbread was also my first experience at baking by eye, not by precise measurement. I wasn't tied down to any cookbook. How much a "dash" or "sprinkle" was, was entirely up to me. I remember gaining the confidence to play with the original cornbread recipe. I added some sugar or took away some shortening, getting it to take on more of my identity. Thinking back, much of that experimentation really came from the mistakes I was making, trying to get the cornbread to taste just like Mom's—maybe even better. It must have been in the middle of all that experimentation, where I was calling some of the taste shots for the cornbread, that I felt a certain link not just with my mother but, through her, with her mother.

First you hurry to get everything right, then you wait.

None of this tradition protected me from the occasional harsh judgments my earliest baking received from my family. I think it had to do with my constantly trying to attain my mother's level of baking. When my father once admitted my cornbread was on a par with Mom's, well, that meant my mother had done well by me as a teacher.

I must have been around thirteen years old when I learned how to make scratch biscuits. They were to become a staple of our weekday meals. Biscuits were particularly good with fried liver, one of the regular things I made during the week. In general, Mom kept the biscuit recipe simple. She knew she was dealing with a young, blossoming daughter whose hormones were bouncing off the wall. She was lucky I was able to concentrate on the simple recipes at all!

But if there was any early baking recipe of my mother's that loomed large, it was her pancake batter. I so wanted to master it, but it resisted for a long time. By age thirteen I was ready to deal with this surprisingly temperamental recipe. That one little recipe taught me so much about simple kitchen technique. I learned about precise stove temperature, about how patient one had to be in not flipping the thick batter prematurely—but that was the most fun, so it was hard to resist. Of course, if I did turn the pancakes too quickly, I had to learn about damage control as I repaired a broken pancake.

My tenth birthday party in my brand-new emerald-green dress

I suppose that simple recipe for pancakes ended up teaching me volumes about the virtues of waiting—waiting and watching for that key moment when those little bubbles slowly rippled the batter's surface, telling me I could slide the spatula underneath a newborn pancake.

If I had to circle with a kind of spiritual Magic Marker my arrival as a real baker, at least in the eyes of my critical family, it probably would be that long-ago Thanksgiving dinner when my mother asked me to make the cornbread for the turkey stuffing. That was a big compliment to me at the ripe old age of seventeen. If I hadn't actually arrived at that point, I was certainly on my way.

My mom was an excellent cook, and I will always take my hat off to her. The proof of her staying power as my teacher is that even after I ventured out on my own as an established baker, I still called her up to ask for recipes. Whenever I wanted something new or special, or just wanted her advice on a problem—any problem—she was just a phone call away.

I remember one time when I had to do a carrot wedding cake, and the customers wanted it with champagne glass tiers. But I had a problem: how to secure the glasses so that they wouldn't flip out from the cake layers as the cake was being cut. Calmly, sensibly, my mother recommended I set the glasses on cardboard pastry layers and "cement" them in place using cake icing. Now my mother wasn't even a professional baker, but her idea was so simple and so full of common sense that it worked perfectly.

The basics taught by the master have stayed with me always.

Muffins

Lemon Poppy Seed Muffins

When it came to flavoring this lemon poppy seed muffin, I wanted to make something that tasted authentic. And I didn't want to add food coloring to the batter, creating the impression that genuine lemons are bright yellow. I mean, when you squeeze a lemon, what do you get? You get a translucent liquid that doesn't really have a color but is cloudy, not bright yellow. Not only do I put lemon juice in the muffins, but I also add lemon extract, a very clear liquid. Combined with flour and eggs, they don't show up bright yellow.

Lemon poppy seed muffins that look real are not in any of the stores. I think what is commercially done feels so "cake boxy." Who are the manufacturers of these muffins trying to fool? Personally, I know when I'm eating a boxed product. And everybody else knows as well. You know when something has been processed. But when the "real deal" crosses our palate, our brain says this is the "real deal." You then say, "I haven't had this since my grandmother or mother made it." It's as if we haven't tasted anything like it because people don't make it anymore.

I get my poppy seeds from the health food store — only the best.

2 cups flour

1 cup sugar

1 tablespoon baking powder

1 teaspoon salt

2 eggs

¼ cup oil

4 tablespoons butter or margarine,
  melted

¾ cup milk

1 teaspoon lemon juice

1 teaspoon corn syrup

1 teaspoon vanilla extract

1 tablespoon lemon extract

2 tablespoons poppy seeds

Preheat the oven to 350 degrees. Combine and sift the flour, sugar, baking powder, and salt. Make a well and place in it the eggs, oil, butter, milk, lemon juice, corn syrup, and vanilla and lemon extracts. Blend by hand, then fold in the poppy seeds. Spoon into a wax paper–lined 12-unit muffin pan and bake for 25 minutes.

❖ *Yield: twelve 2–4-ounce muffins or six 6–8-ounce muffins*

Morning Glory Muffins

This was truly a creation born of necessity. I had a little bit of carrot, a little bit of apple, some pineapple, and a lot of walnuts. I needed another muffin "flavor of the day," and money was tight. Since I couldn't buy additional supplies, I made the muffin with the ingredients I had.

I hauled out a bowl and started dicing and chopping up the apples (with peels) and grating the carrots, and I rescued some of the pineapple from the piña colada muffins. Using the apple peel is a story in and of itself. The peel is the most valuable part of the apple, and for the longest time I had been discarding it. Then a fellow chef pointed out how much money, not to mention vitamins, was going from my peeler into the trash.

As for the name, it might just as easily have been called "everything but the kitchen sink" for all the ingredients it had. But my assistant wondered if she would have to handwrite on every muffin label that this was a "walnut, carrot, pineapple, apple" creation, so I came up with the name Morning Glory after the beautiful, bright yellow–budded flower that seemed to sum up the brightness of this muffin's flavors.

In my experimental mode

2 cups flour

2 teaspoons baking powder

1 teaspoon baking soda

1 teaspoon salt

½ teaspoon cinnamon

½ teaspoon nutmeg

¼ teaspoon mace

2 carrots, grated

1 apple, grated

1 cup oil

1 cup sugar

2 eggs

¼ cup crushed pineapple

¼ cup chopped nuts

Preheat the oven to 350 degrees. Sift together the dry ingredients. Place the carrots, apple, oil, and sugar in a bowl and mix with an electric mixer until well blended. Add the eggs one at a time. Gradually add the dry mixture. Fold in the pineapple and nuts. Spoon into a wax paper–lined 12-unit muffin pan and bake for 30–35 minutes.

❖ *Yield: twelve 2–4-ounce muffins or six 6–8-ounce muffins*

Quick Breads

Date Nut Bread

This recipe goes back at least thirty years, when I was in my "Suzy Homemaker" early baking days. I was always trying to find new ways to experiment with my baked goods, always adapted from the recipes buried in my mother's cookbooks. This recipe also reminds me of my days as a kid when you could buy that little eight-ounce can of date nut bread. I was dying to make my own date nut bread so that I wouldn't have to content myself with the few servings one got from the store-bought version.

This particular bread is really like a fruitcake, but without all that hard, citrusy stuff. Keep in mind, dates are expensive but they are great. I just love their flavor.

The orange juice used here is just for flavoring and some moisture, not that you need a whole lot of moisture with this recipe. Dates, like a lot of fruit, give off their own moisture. When this bread is baked, the moisture is released into the flour. Although they are much more expensive, you can use pecans instead of walnuts.

For the bread
1 cup fresh dates
¾ cup sugar
10½ tablespoons butter or
    margarine
2 cups flour
2½ teaspoons baking powder
1 teaspoon salt

¼ teaspoon mace
2 eggs, beaten
1 cup milk
1½ teaspoons vanilla extract
½ cup finely chopped walnuts
For the orange juice glaze
½ cup brown sugar, packed
½ cup orange juice

Preheat the oven to 350 degrees. Chop the dates into pieces. Cream the sugar and butter, and add the dates. Sift the flour with the baking powder, salt, and mace. Alternately add the eggs, flour mixture, and milk to the creamed mix. Add the vanilla. Fold in the walnuts. Pour into a 4 by 8-inch loaf pan. Bake for 45 minutes to 1 hour.

To make the glaze, boil the brown sugar and orange juice for 3 minutes. Pour over the cake immediately after removing it from the oven.

❖ *Yield: 8–12 servings*

Nut Loaf

When I am inspired to do something with a lot of nuts, I'm thinking about all those trips my family made down to North Carolina, through Virginia, passing by those Stuckey's eateries on the way. Unfortunately, it was the 1950s and Jim Crowism was still very much in effect. I never understood why my parents never wanted to stop as we made our way south. All I could do was imagine what one of those Stuckey's pecan rolls tasted like.

Left to right: my friend Cheryl, me, and my sister Brenda

The pecan tree in my aunt's yard in Merry Hill, North Carolina, just showered pecans, making them really appealing to me from my earliest youth. I remember how each year my aunt used to give away so many of those nuts to the family, including making her own fruitcakes as Christmas gifts. That whole North Carolina experience was real country to me. It was a place where you could watch a chicken being killed that morning and have it served up at the next meal.

The black walnuts used in this recipe have more flavor to them than regular walnuts. They are a mapley, richer-tasting nut. The outer skin of the meat is black, not the shell. And the meat itself, white on the inside, has a sweeter taste to it—again, like maple sugar.

¼ *pound (1 stick) butter*
¼ *pound margarine*
1½ *cups sugar*
4 eggs
1 teaspoon vanilla extract

1 teaspoon salt
¾ *teaspoon baking powder*
1 cup milk
1 cup black walnut pieces
1 cup pecan pieces

Cream the butter, margarine, and sugar until light and fluffy. Add the eggs one at a time. Add the vanilla. Sift the dry ingredients and add to the creamed mix, alternating with milk. Fold in the walnut and pecan pieces. Pour into a wax paper–lined 10-inch tube pan. Place in a cold oven and bake at 300 degrees for 1 hour and 40 minutes.

❖ *Yield: 15–20 servings*

Nut Ring

This is one of those recipes pulled from my mother's original collection. In my family we've always loved nuts. Dad had a nut bowl, and it was always filled with hazelnuts, pecans, or walnuts, depending on the time of year. Price had a lot to do with what nuts were in stock; pecans were the most expensive. My father could crack those nuts so easily with a nutcracker. It was always such a task for us girls. That effectively removed some of the temptation to steal them—you had to work so hard. We girls were grateful when Dad tossed us one.

¼ pound (1 stick) butter
1 cup white sugar
2 eggs
2 cups sifted flour
1 teaspoon baking soda
1 teaspoon baking powder
¼ teaspoon mace

½ teaspoon nutmeg
8 ounces sour cream
¾ cup chopped walnuts
1 teaspoon cinnamon
3 tablespoons brown sugar
2 tablespoons melted butter

Preheat the oven to 350 degrees. Cream the solid butter and white sugar. Add the eggs, flour, baking soda, baking powder, mace, nutmeg, and sour cream. Combine the nuts, cinnamon, and brown sugar. Place half of the batter in a wax paper–lined or greased 10-inch tube pan. Top with half of the brown sugar mix. Repeat with the second half of the batter and brown sugar mix. Pour the melted butter on top. Bake for 50 minutes. Let cool before removing from the pan.

❖ *Yield: 15–20 servings*

Peanut Butter Loaf

Peanut butter has always been a staple in my mother's cookbooks. Despite some difficult first experiences with peanut butter cookies so many eons ago, I really love this recipe. I will admit that I didn't dare deal with peanut butter for a long time, but I eventually did not only this recipe but others, including a peanut butter cheesecake.

As peanut butter tends to be on the stiff side, you really need to add butter and/or margarine to make it more pliable and easier to work with. Chunky or smooth, either kind of peanut butter will do. Of course, if you are a nut lover, the chunky one will serve your purposes better.

1 cup sugar	*1 egg*
4 tablespoons butter or margarine	*1 teaspoon vanilla extract*
¼ cup peanut butter	*2 cups flour*
1 cup buttermilk	*1½ teaspoons baking powder*
1 teaspoon baking soda	*Chopped peanuts (optional)*

Preheat the oven to 350 degrees. Cream the sugar, butter, and peanut butter together. Add the buttermilk and baking soda. Add the egg and vanilla. Sift together the flour and baking powder. Combine with the peanut butter mixture. Spoon into a 4 by 8-inch loaf pan. Bake for 40–45 minutes. Sprinkle the chopped peanuts on top of the batter if you are using them.

❖ *Yield: 8–12 servings*

Pecan Loaf

I just love pecans. They are so sweet, but with a distinctive taste to them. Walnuts can be waxy, whereas pecans have a nicer, woodsier taste. They are just plain good.

I remember the famous Stuckey's pecan roll they used to sell—perhaps they still do. My feeling was that a pecan loaf would bring back the taste of what Stuckey's had.

Here I am at five giving a little impromptu performance.

As for toasting pecans, you can spread them on a tray and toast them for 15 minutes at 350 degrees. This gives them a nuttier flavor. It's worth trying.

½ pound (2 sticks) butter or margarine
2 cups sugar
4 eggs
4 cups flour
2 teaspoons baking powder

¼ teaspoon nutmeg
1 teaspoon salt
1 cup milk
2 teaspoons vanilla extract
2½ cups pecans, toasted

Preheat the oven to 350 degrees. Cream the butter and sugar. Add the eggs one at a time. Sift together the flour, baking powder, nutmeg, and salt. Add alternately with milk to the creamed mixture. Add the vanilla. Fold in the pecans. Bake in two 4 by 8-inch loaf pans for 45 minutes.

❖ *Yield: 8–12 servings*

Pecan Tarts

For these tarts it is advisable to use a standard two- to three-ounce-capacity twelve-unit muffin pan. Don't fill the individual molds up all the way with dough. That will not leave enough room for the rest of the filling. What you will produce, if all goes well, is a mini-pecan pie without all that gluelike stickiness. Normally, I love pecans in everything, but I find standard pecan pie just too sweet.

For the tart
¼ pound (1 stick) butter, softened
3 ounces cream cheese, softened
1 cup flour
½ cup chopped pecans

For the filling
¾ cup brown sugar, packed
1 egg
1 teaspoon vanilla extract
1 tablespoon butter
⅓ cup chopped pecans

Cream the butter and cream cheese. Add the flour. Chill. Shape into 1-inch balls. Place the balls in muffin pans and press to create tart shells. Sprinkle the ½ cup nuts in the shells. Preheat the oven to 350 degrees. To make the filling, beat the sugar, egg, vanilla, and butter until smooth. Sprinkle the ⅓ cup nuts on top of the filling. Bake in an ungreased 12-unit muffin pan for 25 minutes. Loosen with a knife and let cool.

❖ Yield: 12 servings

Cookies and Pastries

Marble Walnut Brownies

This particular creation comes from my son, Olivier. When he was an infant, I would keep him in his stroller in the kitchen. One day I was working on this cookie dough, and Olivier distracted me. Somehow I ended up dumping everything into one bowl. It was a classic "Oops, I didn't mean to do that" moment. At the same time it was really too late to take it back.

I remember looking at the mess in the bowl and thinking, What have I done? And what was I going to do? What could I say to a baby? So I decided to work it out. I took my spatula and spread out the new creation over a pan. They were originally supposed to be cookies for an official cookie order that was due. So I baked the whole thing

Your mistakes can lead you to new flavor combinations.

and took it to my customers. They bought it gladly. Suddenly "Olivier's Brownies" were born.

They resemble those white brownies called "blondies." The marbleizing comes from throwing everything into the bowl at the same time, mixing the chocolate, walnuts, and chocolate chips. When you scrape it out and spread it in a pan, it starts to marbleize itself.

It was a great lesson—you can always make something out of what appears to be a disaster.

2 cups flour
1½ cups sugar
1 teaspoon baking powder
½ teaspoon salt
½ pound (2 sticks) butter or
  margarine

2 eggs
2 teaspoons vanilla extract
6 tablespoons cocoa
3 tablespoons oil
1 cup chocolate chips
1 cup chopped walnuts

Preheat the oven to 350 degrees. Combine the flour, sugar, baking powder, and salt. Cut the butter into the flour mix. Make a well and add the eggs and vanilla. Mix by hand. Combine the cocoa and oil to form a paste. Pour or spoon the paste on top of the dough. Do not mix. Add the chocolate chips and walnuts. Spoon into a greased 9 by 13-inch pan. Using a spatula, spread the mixture in the pan. Blend it in until it looks marbled. Bake for 25–30 minutes.

❖ *Yield: 8–12 servings*

Fruits

Ninth-grade photo, age fifteen. My mother gave me these earrings, even though she didn't want my ears pierced.

When I was becoming a young woman, I think the operative adjective to describe me would be "wild." I spent a good deal of my teenage years saying a lot of "nay, nay, nay." I was a rebel without a cause. I was bold and bodacious and, to top it all off, probably owing to my short stature, I had a serious "little man" syndrome. I had one of the bigger mouths of the neighborhood for someone so small.

Later on, as I developed into a baker, I think my irreverent attitude came out in going in the opposite direction of the haute cuisine everyone was looking for. I dared to go back to the basics, in the hope of touching on what the public really wanted, not the artificial stuff being sold commercially.

Going back to those combustible teen years, truth be told, I did my best to toe the family line—so I wasn't really all that rebellious. But my mother always said I was more Barnes—my father's side of the family. And my father's side was where you could find the wild ones and the entrepreneurial ones, too. I'm sure I got my drive from their side. In general, though, my parents were always quite liberal-thinking people, so they gave my siblings and me a lot of rope—certainly enough to hang ourselves.

As a teenager I had to balance my emerging creative self with the fact that, as the senior child, I was caught up in the domestic stuff I had to do. I wanted to help my mother with her chores. Yet there was clearly another part of me that, by the time I reached eighteen, wanted so badly to leave the house.

Falling in love with a childhood sweetheart—really a knight in shining armor of the tall, dark, and handsome variety—was an unstated goal

Senior prom with the man who would become my first husband

of mine. At that point I was happy to become a homemaker, wife, and have children. I mean, that's what I saw in the movies every week, those happily-ever-after endings. As a teenager I wanted happily-ever-after. I wanted the ideal of *Leave It to Beaver* and *Father Knows Best* and all the other homespun television shows that my parents approved of. In fact, probably by the time I was twelve, I had already planned on being married by the time I reached eighteen.

Sure enough, I did end up with the great jock of a rival high school. We were the ideal couple, living that television lifestyle, driving around in a 1967 fire-engine-red Mustang. We married when I was eighteen, and as I became a housewife, I found myself consulting often with my mother. In those years I still took so many of my cues from her. She was one stylish lady.

In general, from that young adult time, I always liked to be a little bit gaudy. I preferred pants more than skirts. I liked funky jewelry and junky, clunky earrings. My mother also wore big earrings. And I've always liked ornate—preferring more rather than less—jewelry. Give me gold over silver any day, and certainly yellow gold over white. Against my mother's wishes, I got my ears pierced, which was a big deal at the time. It must have been around 1964, when one of President Johnson's daughters—I think it might have been Lucy—got hers done. Though my mother was vehemently opposed to the ear piercing, she still bought me my first pair of real gold earrings.

The owner of this jewelry store always buys a bun from me—he says it makes his morning.

Looking at my baking attire today, I think my old funkiness still colors my wardrobe. In the kitchen I've dressed to follow my own instincts, to set my own style. Let's see, in the wintertime I wear Moon thermal boots, blue jeans, a black shirt, gold hoop earrings, and, of course, a print scarf for a hair net.

I really think that at times I see two separate classes tugging away at me. My middle-class upbringing and education are occasionally at odds with the blue-collar sweat of my life as a professional baker. Mind you, I have no problems admitting that I'm a blue-collar worker. I think I've always done what I damn well please.

From the earliest time I can remember, I loved to draw—first with crayons, later with pencils. I remember loving the challenge of staying within the confines of the coloring book's designs.

We had a lot of original art pieces in our house, including several by a successful commercial artist. He loved to home in on one bit of nature, like one iris—not a field of them, mind you—and just enlarge that bit of nature. Seeing that this man, who was the main designer for all the artwork for a big local grocery store, could make a living as an artist—well, I'm sure that got me thinking that art could be an avenue for me as well.

So even though my parents had other ideas about what I could do with my education, thinking more along the lines of my becoming a doctor or lawyer, I never let art stray from my ambitious sights. Later on, already into my first marriage, I enrolled in George Washington University's art program, taking commercial and graphic design courses at the Corcoran Gallery. I still avidly collect poster reproductions by Monet, Gauguin, and Wyeth. I still have an easel in the middle of my living room.

As art became more and more a part of me, an extension of who I was as a person, baking assumed a similar role. As with a work of art, it was so wonderful after having baked something to point to it and say, "I did that." There is something about creating anything with your own bare hands and then reaping the satisfaction from the creation that you did all by yourself. Also, it has given me tremendous satisfaction knowing that people enjoy what I bake. Like praise for a creative work of art, it is always a great boost to my sense of self.

Artistically I think most people are afraid to live, are afraid to step out there and express themselves. For me, that expression meant that I was going to step out and do what I pleased, knowing full well that down the road there might be a high price for that.

I know for a fact you don't forget your first love. Likewise, it is difficult for me to forget what first inspired me to treat baking like art. It came from the most unassuming of sources: those beat-up church bazaar cookbooks that my mother collected and eventually passed on

The joy of hand-mixing

to me. If there was one lesson those old texts taught me, it was that even the everyday muffin should never be just ho-hum.
There is a rainbow of flavors available.

I often devised a new flavor for a muffin or cupcake just for the sake of changing pace. Chalk it up to restless, artistic creativity. Also, the seasons have a powerful influence on which new flavors I pursue for my muffins, cupcakes, and quick breads. What is most readily available when I look in the larder of my kitchen or at the corner store? If the time is right, I'll pounce on the ripest raspberries, strawberries, and peaches.

I've found that some produce is cooperative all year round. Always available are the reliable apple, the banana, and the blueberry (which, by the by, is the most popular muffin stuffer on the market). And then there is the very versatile cranberry—which comes up in my Cran-Orange Muffins. The great little secret about the humble cranberry is that not only does it keep very well frozen, but it actually bakes better frozen than fresh.

A lot of my baking ideas come when I'm running short of an ingredient. I find myself just grabbing what I have, switching things around, and making it work well in a new form. It may seem whimsical, but necessity has always been my primary mother of invention.

I think making these flavors up as you go along is what anyone who possesses real creativity does. A real artist is someone who can work without all the accoutrements or without the net of a recipe. If you have to have it all, you're not the genuine article. A real pro makes do and really improvises, letting his or her imagination do the work.

Of course, you have to work with the freshest, boldest-flavored ingredients in order to make the art of baking come alive. My mother never skimped on fresh ingredients in her baked goods, and I feel that I would almost be doing her a disservice if I didn't carry on that part of her culinary legacy.

The response I'm looking for is "I've never seen or tasted that before in a muffin or cupcake." It shouldn't surprise anyone when I come up with a piña colada or a peach cobbler muffin.

What you'll find most often in stores today is really a prefab, "plastified" muffin, and it really suffers in comparison with something that is home-baked. The raspberry muffin seems to tell it all. The traditional store-bought raspberry muffin will have a dab of raspberry puree in its doughy middle. But, honestly, I've never actually seen a real live raspberry in the middle of any one of those store-bought muffins. It's been reduced to nothing more than a kind of reddish hue in the bread. You get the flavor, sort of, but where is the fruit?

People want to see the fruit, because if they don't see it, they feel they are getting ripped off. They start to think that maybe a bottle of raspberry juice just leaked into the middle of the muffin.

I like ingredients that present themselves boldly and in profusion. Getting back to the raspberry, I adore its distinctive taste combination of both tart and, when mixed with sugar, sweet. I mean fresh raspberries are as puckery as lemons, so the taste of a raspberry can be both bold and subtle. In my raspberry muffin, when it comes out right, you get the immediate mix of the sweet and sour, the tart and sugary coming together. It really demands your attention. It's announcing, "I'm here. This is me, I'm out here, and you can taste it." I think that's why I've always partially identified with the raspberry's bold taste. I also like its burgundy color, the color of royalty. I think I've always considered myself a bit of an "African Queen" anyway.

Then there are my chocolate and white chocolate muffins. I mean, they are chock-full of whole chunks of chocolate. Most commercial products have a little smear of chocolate in them. My muffins aren't shy about it.

When you eat one of these muffins and compare it with what you find at a grocery store, the difference is immediately apparent.

Apple dumpling muffins

Muffins

Apple Dumpling Muffins

This recipe is a prime example of having—or, more to the point, not having—a piece of kitchen equipment determine what kind of creative muffin to enjoy. Lacking my electric shredder, I had to hand-slice the apples. That meant the slices of apple would be very obvious in the interior of the muffin—hardly a loss by any means.

You can see the slices in the muffin, and when you bite into one, there they are. It's a little like the sensation of eating an apple pie. You've cooked the raw apples down, but you can still see them. A real apple dumpling is a whole apple, peel and all, wrapped in pastry or dough before being baked in the oven. Well, this apple dumpling muffin works on the same principle. A whole apple has been sliced and is subsequently surrounded by dough or batter.

I knew that customers were used to having their apples shredded and were used to the different texture that imparts. I was in a bit of a bind because I could not market sliced apples under the "apple nut" label, since the apple nut texture is much smoother, thanks to the shredded apples. So I decided to slice the apples, kick out the walnuts used in the apple nut, and change the name. That's what we call "necessity of the moment" creativity.

2 cups flour
1 cup sugar
1 tablespoon baking powder
1 teaspoon salt
½ teaspoon cinnamon
¼ teaspoon mace
¼ teaspoon cardamom
⅛ teaspoon ground cloves

¼ cup oil
4 tablespoons butter or margarine,
  melted
2 eggs
¾ cup milk
2 apples, peeled, cored, and cut
  into slices

Preheat the oven to 350 degrees. Sift together all the dry ingredients. Make a well in the center and mix in by hand the oil, butter, eggs, and milk. Fold in the sliced apples. Spoon into a wax paper–lined 12-unit muffin pan. Bake for 30–35 minutes.

❖ Yield: twelve 2–4-ounce muffins or six 6–8-ounce muffins

Apple Nut Muffins

The first thing to note with this recipe is that for it and for any other recipe involving apples, I recommend using Granny Smiths. After having tried Golden Delicious and other varieties, I found nothing really matches Granny Smith apples for their combination of tartness and sturdiness when baked.

This recipe also brings out the distinction between grating and dicing apples. A grated apple is better able to blend into the mix. Dicing the apple produces chunks that don't blend as well. Obviously, with a fine grating, there are absolutely no chunks of apple. For this recipe, a finer gauge is necessary, while dicing is needed for the Apple Crumb Nut Muffins. For that recipe you should use diced apples because you want the apple to be seen in the cake, since it's competing with an all-but-overwhelming crumb topping. People need to know there is some apple there.

But in this muffin the apple is not competing with any other ingredient, so you can get away with grating it.

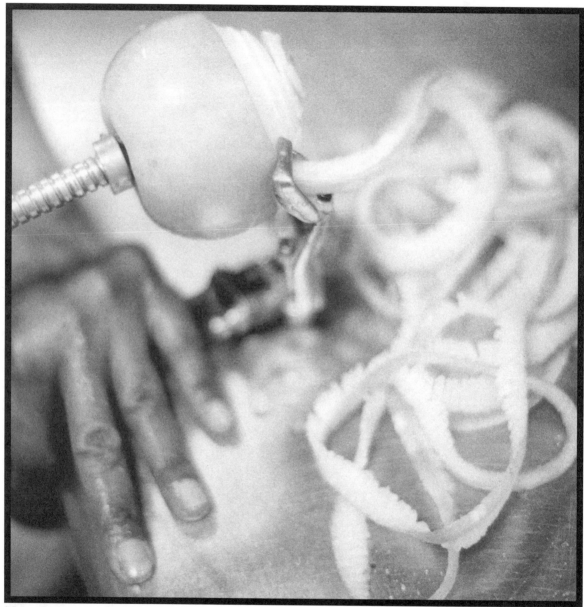

This apple corer doubles as a slicer and a peeler.

2 cups flour

1 cup sugar

1 tablespoon baking powder

1 teaspoon salt

1/2 teaspoon cinnamon

1/4 teaspoon mace

1/4 teaspoon cardamom

1/8 teaspoon ground cloves

1/4 cup oil

1/4 pound (1 stick) butter or
    margarine, melted

3/4 cup milk

2 medium-size apples, grated

1/2 cup chopped walnuts

Preheat the oven to 350 degrees. Combine all the dry ingredients. Make a well in the center. Add the remaining ingredients except the apples and walnuts. Mix by hand. Add the apples and walnuts, and mix in. Spoon into a wax paper–lined 12-unit muffin pan. Bake for 30 minutes.

Variation: Add 1/2 cup of raisins.
....

❖ *Yield: Twelve 2–4-ounce muffins or six 6–8-ounce muffins*

Banana Nut Muffins

For the banana nut muffin, I decided that just a little bit of mace would heighten and shape the already pungent aroma that bananas—especially very ripe ones—give off. What is mace? It is nutmeg—specifically, the scratchings of the hull of the nutmeg shell. Open up any nutmeg, and there is always a bit of powdery residue on the inside. Scraped off, that powder is more pungent than the actual nutmeg meat itself. Whenever a recipe calls for nutmeg, you could use half as much mace and get the exact same result.

Mace is an accentuator. It is especially useful in cakes or pies where fruit is used. To everything from pumpkin to carrot, mace brings its special enhancing qualities. It has almost an intoxicating effect.

Mace is a powerful spice, and too much of it will ruin the intended taste. When it is used sparingly, everybody who tastes it tends to love it. A little mace in a pound cake, and it suddenly becomes a hot-selling item. Someone recently tasted my banana nut muffin and immediately guessed I had put mace in it—and there was so little!

Also notice that the baking soda and baking powder both act as leavening ingredients, with the baking soda in

Christine looks happy after buying a banana nut muffin.

particular giving a definite taste and color to this and other baked items. People may not realize it, but baking soda tends to brown; it makes your dish brown on the inside. It's great for chocolate and spice cakes, making them a deeper umber. It also augments and works well with buttermilk and sour cream.

2–3 ripe bananas	*1 teaspoon baking soda*
1 cup oil	*1 teaspoon salt*
2 eggs	*¼ teaspoon mace*
1 cup sugar	*1 teaspoon vanilla extract*
2 cups flour	*½ cup chopped nuts*
2 teaspoons baking powder	

Preheat the oven to 350 degrees. Place the bananas in a mixing bowl and beat with an electric mixer until pureed or mashed. Add the oil and sugar. Add the eggs one at a time. Sift the dry ingredients. Gradually add the sifted ingredients. Add the vanilla. Fold in the nuts. Bake in a wax paper–lined 12-unit muffin pan for 30–35 minutes.

Variation: Sprinkle chocolate chips on top of the batter before baking.

❖ *Yield: Twelve 2–4-ounce muffins or six 6–8-ounce muffins*

Blueberry—the king of muffins

Blueberry Muffins

It's clear that the minute you say muffins, the first thought is blueberry. I don't pretend to understand the history of it, but it remains a classic of the field. It's odd how for all its apparent simplicity, it can still stump some master bakers I've worked with.

One master baker at Catholic University couldn't make a blueberry muffin to save his life. When I first started out, before using my mother's pancake recipe, I instinctively leaned toward the next best thing, which was a muffin mix. While the other chefs were contenting themselves with a cake mix, the muffin mix was just right to support something weighty besides the standard flour, sugar, and eggs. A juicy blueberry has so much juice, in fact, that oftentimes it will explode while baking. You need a heavy batter to absorb the juice and not allow the berry to sink to the bottom.

Freezing the blueberries also prevents them from sinking. When you drop some frozen fruit into the batter, it immediately makes the batter freeze up and cling more to the fruit. By the time the fruit starts to break down in the baking process, the batter is turning into its new solid bread form, supporting the blueberries even better.

Another thing about the blueberry muffin is that the blueberries are more fragile than they appear. If you go charging into the batter with a mixer, the berries will bleed and the muffins will come out blue. So freezing the blueberries before adding them to the batter also helps avoid the excessive bleeding of juice.

4 rounded cups flour
2 cups sugar
2 tablespoons baking powder
2 teaspoons salt
4 eggs
½ cup oil

1 stick tablespoons butter or
 margarine, melted
1½ cups milk
2 teaspoons vanilla extract
16 ounces frozen blueberries or
 1 pint fresh berries

Preheat the oven to 350 degrees. Sift together all the dry ingredients. Make a well in the center. Add the eggs, oil, butter, milk, and vanilla. Gently hand-mix until all the liquid is absorbed. Fold in the blueberries. Using an 8-ounce ice cream scoop, place 1 scoop of batter into each unit of a large, wax paper–lined 12-unit muffin pan (or two 6-unit muffin pans). Bake for 30–40 minutes, depending on the doneness of the muffins in the center of the tin. When you press against the tops of the muffins, they should be firm to the touch.

❖ *Yield: One dozen 6-ounce muffins*

Blueberry muffins ready to go into the oven

Cran-Orange Muffins

I just love cranberry juice and cranberry sauce. I know the cranberry season almost by heart. It's painfully short, lasting from the beginning of September through December, with its peak during October into late November. That's it. It is difficult to find whole fresh cranberries after December. The reason is that cranberries are grown like rice, in marshy areas, which complicates their harvest.

Jellied cranberry sauce just doesn't cut it. When I developed a muffin, it was with the idea that it could be made only seasonally, in autumn when the fresh whole cranberries were available. When they first arrive in the grocery stores, I all but leap at them.

Combining the assertive tartness of the cranberry with the subtle quality of the orange adds up to a very distinctive autumnal flavor.

2 cups flour
1 cup sugar
1 tablespoon baking powder
1 teaspoon salt
¼ teaspoon mace
2 eggs
¼ cup oil

¼ cup melted butter or margarine
¾ cup milk
1 teaspoon vanilla extract
2 teaspoons orange extract
¼ cup orange marmalade
6 ounces whole fresh cranberries

Preheat the oven to 350 degrees. Sift together all the dry ingredients. Make a well in the center. Add the eggs, oil, butter, milk, and vanilla and orange extracts. Blend by hand. Mix in the orange marmalade and cranberries. Spoon into a wax paper–lined 12-unit muffin pan. Bake for 30–35 minutes.

❖ *Yield: twelve 2–4-ounce muffins or six 6–8-ounce muffins*

Peach Cobbler Muffins

I used to do a plain peach muffin with fresh peaches grown in a friend's orchard in Carroll County, Maryland. I enjoy hoarding those peaches and freezing them so that in the summer, well past their peak season, I can cut them up and mix them in with my muffin mix at any time.

One customer suggested that if I added some cinnamon to my regular peach muffin, it would become a peach cobbler—and it's true. I love cinnamon on peaches and it immediately does conjure up that homey peach cobbler flavor.

Note this recipe's use of two unripe peaches. When they are baked in the oven, the heat ripens them up almost instantly. While the peaches are freezing, you can prepare the other ingredients. Later, when they are frozen, you can peel and slice them more easily (Frankly, the best and most easily sliced kind of peach for this kind of baking is a firm, hard peach. A soft, overripe peach is the best one to freeze.) You place large sections of peach in the center of the batter, then sprinkle cinnamon on top of the batter.

You can see the fruit in these peach cobbler muffins.

It's important that the peaches be sliced as opposed to cut into chunks. One lesson I've learned is that peaches cut into pieces, once they are baked, shrivel up, as apple chunks will. But peach slices placed in the center of the batter won't get lost. When a person bites into this muffin anywhere, it is there, and you can't miss it.

2 firm peaches
2 cups flour
1 cup sugar
1 tablespoon baking powder
1 teaspoon salt
4 tablespoons butter or margarine,
  melted

¼ cup oil
¾ cup milk
1 teaspoon vanilla extract
Cinnamon (for dusting)

Preheat the oven to 350 degrees. Peel and slice the peaches into 6 parts per peach. Sift together the dry ingredients. Make a well in the center. Add the butter, oil, milk, and vanilla. Blend by hand. Spoon the batter into a wax paper–lined 12-unit muffin pan. Insert peach wedges (2 per muffin). Dust freely with cinnamon. Bake for 30–35 minutes, or until the center of each muffin is resistant to touch.

❖ *Yield: twelve 2–4-ounce muffins or six 6–8-ounce muffins*

Piña Colada Muffins

I remember one day having a little bit of pineapple and a teensy bit of coconut. That was all I had on hand, and that was how it hit me to try a piña colada muffin.

I toasted the coconut because I'm a baker, and any baker worth his salt knows that coconut's flavor is enhanced when you toast it first. I remember a colleague of mine with a lot of kitchen experience who thought she could toast coconut by spreading it out in a pan and sticking it underneath an industrial-strength broiler. Well, the flames that shot up from her pan confirmed what I already knew. Coconut, with its high sugar content, is incredibly flammable. The safe way to toast coconut is to put it on a cookie sheet in an oven set at 350 degrees for around 10 minutes. You need to check it periodically because coconut burns easily.

You can also add some rum flavoring to this muffin, to really make it like the piña colada drink.

4 ounces toasted, flaked coconut
2 cups flour
1 cup sugar
1 tablespoon baking powder
1 teaspoon salt
2 eggs
3/4 cup milk

1/4 cup oil
4 tablespoons butter or margarine, melted
1 teaspoon vanilla extract
1/3 cup crushed pineapple (in its own juice, not in heavy syrup)

Preheat the oven to 350 degrees. Toast the coconut for 10 minutes or until browned. Sift together all the dry ingredients. Blend in the eggs, milk, oil, butter, and vanilla. Fold in the coconut and pineapple. Spoon into a wax paper–lined 12-unit muffin pan and bake for 30 minutes.

❖ *Yield: twelve 2–4-ounce muffins or six 6–8-ounce muffins*

Don't you just want to lick the spoon?

Raspberry Muffins

I simply adore raspberries. At first, a raspberry has a flavor, and then it hits you hard with a very distinctive tartness. It blends wonderfully with chocolate, yet it makes a statement by itself. There is something appealing, verging on the seductive, about raspberries.

I prefer to use frozen raspberries, since not only are they more economical but also they hold up better in the batter.

A twelve-ounce bag of frozen raspberries will provide for two dozen regular-size or a dozen oversize muffins. Any leftover raspberries can be spread on cake layers for a wonderful dessert icing. With raspberries, everyone is guaranteed to "oooh" and "ahhhh."

2 cups flour
1 cup sugar
1 tablespoon baking powder
1 teaspoon salt
2 eggs
¼ cup oil
4 tablespoons butter or margarine,
*   melted*

¾ cup milk
1 teaspoon vanilla extract
6 ounces fresh raspberries or
*   6 ounces unsweetened frozen*
*   raspberries*

Preheat the oven to 350 degrees. Sift together the dry ingredients. Blend in the eggs, oil, butter, milk, and vanilla. Fold in the berries. Place in a wax paper–lined 12-unit muffin pan. Bake for 35–40 minutes.

❖ *Yield: twelve 2–4-ounce muffins or six 6–8-ounce muffins*

Red, White, and Blue Muffins

The July 4th celebration gave me the idea for this muffin. Oddly enough, from a marketing standpoint, it didn't go over too well because nobody knew what the colors stood for in terms of food.

The blue is for blueberries, the red is for raspberries, and the white comes from the muffin's interior itself. It is a very tasty muffin and frankly could be a year-round item.

What the red, white, and blue muffin did teach me, though, is that people are a bit cautious at trying new things. They want to be familiar with the tastes they are trying in a muffin. Peach cobbler, blueberry, and chocolate chip are all things they can relate to. But when a muffin has an unfamiliar name, the consumer isn't sure he or she wants to be that daring.

Raspberries are one of my favorite fruits.

2 cups flour
1 cup sugar
1 tablespoon baking powder
1 teaspoon salt
2 eggs
¼ cup oil
4 tablespoons butter or margarine,
   melted

¾ cup milk
1 teaspoon vanilla extract
⅛ teaspoon mace (optional)
½ cup blueberries
½ cup raspberries

Preheat the oven to 350 degrees. Sift together the dry ingredients. Make a well in the center. Add the eggs, oil, butter, milk, vanilla, and mace, if you are using it. Blend by hand. Fold in the blueberries and raspberries. Bake in a wax paper–lined 12-unit muffin pan for 35–40 minutes.

❖ *Yield: twelve 2–4-ounce muffins or six 6–8-ounce muffins*

Strawberry-Cream Muffin

This muffin must rank as my all-time favorite. I just love strawberries, yet I found that in a muffin alone they simply weren't selling at all. So I came up with this idea because I truly love strawberries mixed with heavy cream and sprinkled with sugar. To me it's like ambrosia.

I can't use real cream in a muffin, of course, because it will dissipate in the batter while it bakes. But I hit upon the idea of using cream cheese. I had to play with it for a while, changing the order of when I added the cream cheese and the strawberries to the batter. I finally arrived at the right order, which was to put the strawberries in first and then pipe the cream cheese on top.

I remember first trying to dice the strawberries, but they disintegrated too rapidly in the batter. It became a matter of leaving the strawberries whole and shoving them into the middle of the batter. Although they burst when heated in the oven, all the juice ended up concentrated in one area.

As for the cream cheese, after it's creamed with an electric mixer, it should be piped into the batter. If a pastry bag isn't available, then the best alternative is to take a plastic sandwich bag and cut off the corner with a pair of scissors. That small hole will simulate a pastry bag tip. Pipe in enough cream cheese on top of the strawberry so that the cheese pokes through the top of the batter.

2 cups flour

1 cup sugar

1 tablespoon baking powder

1 teaspoon salt

4 tablespoons butter or margarine,
melted

¼ cup oil

¾ cup milk

2 eggs

1 teaspoon vanilla extract

½ pint strawberries

8 ounces cream cheese

Preheat the oven to 350 degrees. Sift together all the dry ingredients. Make a well in the center. Blend in the remaining ingredients except the strawberries and cream cheese. Spoon the batter into a wax paper–lined 12-unit muffin pan. Place 1 or 2 berries in the center of the batter in each muffin mold. Whip the cream cheese and place in a small pastry bag with a number 4 tip. Squeeze about 1 tablespoon of cream cheese into and on top of the strawberries. Bake for 35–40 minutes.

❖ *Yield: twelve 2–4-ounce muffins or six 6–8-ounce muffins*

The batter is poured and waiting for these slices to be added.

Quick Breads

Breakfast Apple Loaf

The apple I use for this and all my recipes is the one and only Granny Smith. Not only is it far and away the best baking apple, but it is so tart that you can easily add sugar to it without making it too sweet. It also remains quite firm while being heated up. With a Granny Smith there is always evidence that an apple is in there.

3 cups flour
1³/₄ cups sugar
1 cup oil
4 eggs
1 tablespoon baking powder

¹/₃ cup orange juice
5 large apples, peeled and sliced
2 teaspoons cinnamon
1 teaspoon nutmeg
Chopped walnuts (optional)

Preheat the oven to 350 degrees. Place the flour, 1½ cups sugar, oil, eggs, baking powder, and orange juice in a bowl and mix well by hand. Mix together the apples, spices, and remaining ¼ cup sugar. Place half of the batter in a wax paper–lined 10-inch tube pan and top with the apple mix. Repeat with the remaining batter and apple mix. The walnuts, if you are using them, may be added on top of the apple mix. Bake for 1 hour.

❖ *Yield: 15–20 servings*

Applesauce Loaf

Everybody has warm feelings when thinking of applesauce and cinnamon together. Apples have a flavor, but they need some seasoning when they are baked. Cardamom, cinnamon, nutmeg, and cloves are key spices with apples, pumpkin, and other autumn fruits. Summer fruits don't need them because they tend to be pungent enough on their own.

¼ pound (1 stick) butter or margarine
1 cup sugar
1 egg
2 cups flour
1 teaspoon salt
1 teaspoon baking soda
1 teaspoon baking powder

1 teaspoon cinnamon
¼ teaspoon cardamom
½ teaspoon nutmeg
¼ teaspoon cloves
1 cup unsweetened applesauce
¾ cup walnuts or pecans, chopped
Confectioners' sugar (for dusting)

Preheat the oven to 350 degrees. Cream together the butter and sugar. Blend in the egg. Sift together the dry ingredients, including the spices. Gradually add to the creamed mixture. Mix in the applesauce and nuts. Bake in a 4 by 8-inch loaf pan for 50 minutes to 1 hour. After cooling, dust with confectioners' sugar.

❖ *Yield: 8–12 servings*

Chewy Apple Loaf

The diced fruit in this loaf gives you all the flavor of the juices and the peel, which carry the essence of the apple.

1½ cups oil

3 eggs

2 cups sugar

2 teaspoons vanilla extract

4 cups flour

1 teaspoon baking soda

2 teaspoons cinnamon

¼ teaspoon cardamom

½ teaspoon salt

3 cups diced apples

1 cup chopped walnuts

Preheat the oven to 350 degrees. Mix together the oil, eggs, sugar, and vanilla at medium speed. Sift together all the dry ingredients. Gradually add to the oil mixture. Fold in the apples and nuts. Bake in two 4 by 8-inch loaf pans for 40–45 minutes.

❖ *Yield: 8–12 servings*

Cranberry Loaf

This is a favorite, since I absolutely love cranberries. This one evolved because I was looking for a fruitcake recipe that didn't have candied fruit in it. I couldn't come up with one, so I found one that could be accommodated to my special needs. I pulled out all the candied fruit and ended up changing the whole darn recipe.

Though this recipe calls for brandy extract, you can use a goodly amount of real brandy in these loaves, as much as half a cup per loaf. Water down the brandy or add sugar to it, then pour it over the loaf after it's done.

I think the mincemeat is a good substitute for candied fruit. People who know that mincemeat is minced beef with currants and sugar added to it might be turned off by it, but I personally like what it does to the flavor of this loaf.

The cranberries explode or shrivel up when they bake. When you slice into this creation, the cranberries are scattered here and there.

1 1/2 cups sugar

6 tablespoons butter

3 eggs

1 teaspoon baking soda

2 cups flour

1/2 teaspoon nutmeg

3/4 teaspoon mace

3/4 cup buttermilk

1/2 package condensed mincemeat or
   1/2 cup mincemeat from a jar

1/4 cup hot water

1 teaspoon brandy extract

1 teaspoon orange extract

2 tablespoons orange marmalade

6 ounces whole fresh cranberries

1/2 cup chopped nuts

Preheat the oven to 350 degrees. Cream together the sugar and butter. Blend in the eggs one at a time. Sift together the dry ingredients. Add them alternately with the buttermilk to the creamed mixture. In a small saucepan, boil the condensed mincemeat in the water; if mincemeat from a jar is used, omit the water. Add the brandy and orange extracts and orange marmalade to the mincemeat. Fold in the mincemeat, cranberries, and nuts. Spoon into a 4 by 8-inch loaf pan. Bake for 45 minutes.

❖ *Yield: 8–12 servings*

Currant Loaf

In terms of flavor, currants have roughly the same qualities as raisins.
What makes this like a fruitcake recipe is the use of candied peels.
These peels are easy to buy in grocery stores. Candied peels from oranges,
lemons, and anything else that has a thick rind can be used. They really
add more color than flavor.

The drizzle icing is for decoration. The best way to drizzle is with a
fork, allowing the icing to drip off in a zigzag pattern. It is easier to do with
a fork than a knife—and safer. A kitchen wire whisk is excellent as well.

¼ pound (1 stick) butter
1 cup sugar
2 eggs, beaten
1 cup sifted flour

⅛ teaspoon mace
1 cup candied peels
1 cup currants

Preheat the oven to 350 degrees. Cream the butter and sugar. Blend
in the eggs. Gradually mix in the flour and mace. Add the peels and currants.
Bake for 45 minutes in an 8 by 8-inch square pan. Ice with "Drizzle Icing"
(recipe follows).

❖ *Yield: 8–12 servings*

"Drizzle Icing"

2 tablespoons water

1 cup confectioners' sugar

Gradually add the water to the sugar until a smooth, thin icing has formed.

Prune Nut Loaf

Growing up, I always loved warm prunes. You start by taking dried prunes and sticking them in a saucepan. Cover them with water and bring to a boil. Turn off the stove and let the prunes sit there, just absorbing the liquid. Put them in a bowl and pour off the juices. I ate these prunes like nobody's business when I was a kid. Even though they might have said prunes were for old folks, I still loved them.

The finished loaf looks like date bread. It really is part of the same family. The nuts in this case are walnuts, but you can also use almonds or pecans.

1 cup sugar
1 cup oil
2 eggs
3 cups flour
1 teaspoon salt
1 teaspoon baking soda
1 teaspoon cinnamon

1 teaspoon nutmeg
¼ teaspoon mace
1 cup buttermilk
1 teaspoon vanilla extract
1 cup chopped cooked prunes
1 cup chopped nuts

Preheat the oven to 350 degrees. Blend the sugar and oil. Add the eggs one at a time. Sift together the dry ingredients. Add alternately with buttermilk to the oil and sugar. Mix in the vanilla, prunes, and nuts. Bake in a 4 by 8-inch loaf pan for 1 hour.

❖ *Yield: 8–12 servings*

Raisin Quick Bread

E veryone seems to have a soft spot for the typical variety of raisin bread. Well, this recipe is a quicker method of getting to the same thing. It goes really well with cream cheese. It's a flavor from my youth and my mother's youth. It's an old classic and a favorite.

16 ounces raisins
2 cups water
1 cup sugar
½ pound (2 sticks) butter or
    margarine

1 teaspoon cinnamon
2½ cups flour
1 teaspoon baking soda
1 teaspoon rum flavoring

Preheat the oven to 350 degrees. Boil the raisins, water, sugar, butter, and cinnamon until the butter is melted. Set aside until cold. Sift together the flour and baking soda. Add gradually to the raisin mixture. Add the rum flavoring. Bake in a greased 10 by 5 by 3-inch loaf pan for 40 to 45 minutes.

❖ Yield: 8–12 servings

Skidmore Loaf

This is a remnant from one of my mother's cookbooks. The fruits and nuts make the loaf a real filler, substantial as well as tasty.

The orange juice over the bread really adds a lot of moisture to the cake and bathes it in orange flavor. These breads are so dense that a lot of the liquid will be absorbed. Remember, since you are dealing with fruits, this loaf should be refrigerated, or you will have a sourdough product on your hands that you won't care for. Unless a bread product with fruit has alcohol in it as a preservative, it will mold pretty quickly.

1 cup sugar
1/3 pound butter or margarine
2 eggs
1 teaspoon baking soda
1 teaspoon baking powder
3 cups flour

1/4 teaspoon mace
1 1/2 cups milk
1 cup raisins
3/4 cup chopped nuts
1 orange, seeded and juiced,
    preserving rind and pulp

Preheat the oven to 350 degrees. Cream the sugar and butter. Blend in the eggs. Sift together all the dry ingredients. Add alternately with milk to the creamed mixture. Fold in the raisins and nuts. In a food processor or blender, grind the orange rind and pulp. Fold into the batter. Bake in a 9 by 13-inch pan for 50 minutes to 1 hour. Pour the orange juice over the hot bread. Cool and serve.

❖ *Yield: 8–12 servings*

Cupcakes and Cakes

Hawaiian Sponge Cake

Pulled from my mother's recipes, this one takes full advantage of crushed pineapple—bringing a lot of moisture to the cake. This makes for a heavy sponge cake, but—remarkably, for a sponge cake—it doesn't fall apart. It has the same type of caramel icing used on German chocolate cake.

For the cake
2 cups flour
1½ cups sugar
1 teaspoon baking soda
¼ teaspoon salt
2 eggs
1 can (20 ounces) crushed
   pineapple in its own juice

For the frosting
¾ cup sugar
¾ cup evaporated milk
¼ pound (1 stick) butter or
   margarine
1 teaspoon vanilla
½ cup nuts, chopped
½ cup coconut, flaked

Preheat the oven to 350 degrees. Combine the dry ingredients. Blend in the eggs and pineapple with its juice. Bake in a 9 by 13-inch pan for 30 minutes. Cool for 10 minutes before frosting.

To make the frosting, combine all the ingredients except the nuts and coconut in a saucepan. Bring to a boil for 7 minutes, or until thickened. Stir in the nuts and coconut.

❖ Yield: 12–15 slices

Holiday Fruitcake

I love using the zest of fruits because it enhances everything, like a time-released flavoring. It is in the peel, after all, that so much flavor hides. When you buy a lemon, you don't have to cut it to smell it. And that wonderful smell is all coming from the peel.

I also like the pineapple and cherries in this fruitcake because they never get hard, even after they have been candied. Nobody I know really likes biting into that hard stuff, and that hard stuff is responsible for Aunt Sarah's fruitcake being left on the shelf along with all the other holiday memorabilia. Every year it seems as if the grocery store just takes its old stock of candied fruit and puts it back on the shelves.

This cake is very rich, but then I've always liked rich desserts. Most people do—even the ones who say they are on a diet.

4 cups flour
1 teaspoon baking powder
½ teaspoon nutmeg
½ teaspoon cinnamon
1 pound (4 sticks) butter or
  margarine
1 pound brown sugar
10 eggs
¼ pound walnuts, chopped
¼ pound pecans, chopped
1 teaspoon lemon zest, finely
  chopped

1 teaspoon orange zest, finely
  chopped
1 pound raisins
¼ pound candied cherries
¼ pound candied pineapple
3 cups sliced and pitted dates
1 cup dark corn syrup
1 cup honey
½ cup orange juice

Preheat the oven to 350 degrees. Line three 4 by 8-inch loaf pans with wax paper. Combine the flour, baking powder, nutmeg, and cinnamon. Sift the mixture. Cream the butter and brown sugar, and beat until light and fluffy. Blend in the eggs, nuts, lemon and orange zests, candied fruits, dates, syrup, honey, and orange juice. Gradually add the dry ingredients. Fill the pans ⅔ full. Bake for 1½ hours. (Hint: A shallow pan of water on the bottom rack of the oven will add moisture during the baking time.) Remove from the oven and cool, covered with a damp cloth.

❖ *Yield: 30 servings*

Honey Fruitcake

This is another recipe from my wonderful mother. Fruitcakes were definitely a holiday treat, especially when Christmas was the holiday. I've always liked fruitcake, but I never, ever liked the hard candied fruit that always comes in it. My mother steered away from that from the beginning. Dried fruits have the same quality as real fruit. When they are baked, you get the feeling the dried fruit was fresh. You don't have to fight with that hard stuff, which can be worse than old chewing gum.

In terms of removing these cakes from the pan, you are dealing with fruit, which is sticky and gives off sugar, and that makes the cakes hard to remove. I don't like adding too much flour and grease to the bottom of the pan, since it really only adds weight to the cake. I prefer to use a double-folded brown paper bag. I cut the bottom off a squared-off paper bag. I then straighten out the whole bag and fold it in half twice. The cut and trimmed bag then fits against the pan's sides. It works like a charm: The cake will lift right off, and you are not fighting with it.

Using a 12-quart bowl for an extra-large batch

2 cups prunes

1 cup dried apricots

1 cup raisins

1 cup slivered blanched almonds

1 cup chopped walnuts

½ pound (2 sticks) butter or
   margarine

1 cup honey

4 eggs

2 cups flour

1 teaspoon salt

1 teaspoon baking powder

1 teaspoon cinnamon

¼ teaspoon cloves

¼ teaspoon mace

½ teaspoon cardamom

Preheat the oven to 350 degrees. Cover the prunes and apricots with boiling water. Drain and cool. Remove pits (if any) from the prunes. Chop the prunes and apricots. Combine the chopped fruit, raisins, almonds, and walnuts. Cream the butter and honey. Add the eggs, beating well after each addition. Sift together the flour, salt, baking powder, and spices. Fold into the creamed mix. Pour the batter over the fruit and nuts. Mix well. Line the bottom and sides of an 8-inch tube pan with 2 layers of a greased brown paper bag (grease the bag by rubbing the end of a stick of margarine over its entire surface) and a layer of wax paper. Pour the mix into the lined pan and bake for 1 hour and 15 minutes.

❖ *Yield: 16–20 servings*

Low-Fat Cake

What makes this cake truly "low-fat" is that it has no eggs or milk. It is my attempt to be accommodating to the low-fat crowd.

This recipe is another remnant from dear Mom. I made this cake during my early "Suzy Homemaker" days. Those were the times, around 1970 and 1971, in the City Line Towers apartment high-rise, when my friends were all housewives, experimenting with cooking and baking. We were constantly giving one another Tupperware parties and baby showers, entertaining each other and guests with these desserts. We were all trying to top each other. It was early in my first marriage, so I was also trying very hard to impress my husband with what I was baking.

During this time I discovered this cake that contained no milk or eggs. I had to try it. Nobody could believe it could be done. It ended up being a little like a fruitcake, with the raisins acting as a binder.

1 cup sugar
1 cup water
1 teaspoon cinnamon
½ teaspoon cloves
1 cup raisins

¼ pound (1 stick) low-fat
  margarine or spread
1 teaspoon baking soda
2 cups flour

Preheat the oven to 350 degrees. Place the sugar, water, cinnamon, cloves, raisins, and margarine in a saucepan. Bring to a boil. Cool and add the baking soda and flour. Pour in a wax paper–lined or greased 9 by 9 by 2-inch pan. Bake for 35 minutes.

❖ *Yield: 12–15 servings*

Orange Fruitcake

My mother simply adored Christmas, and I inherited that love of the holiday from her. My living room, year-round, has little symbols of Christmas tucked in it.

Orange is front and center in this cake. I just love oranges—they enhance the flavor of anything. The dates for this recipe should be pitless. "Dromedary" dates, the brand, are great and they come in exactly the eight-ounce size you need.

½ pound (2 sticks) butter or margarine, softened
3½ cups sugar
4 eggs
4¾ cups flour
2 teaspoons baking soda

1⅓ cups buttermilk
2 cups chopped walnuts
1 8-ounce package dates
1 cup orange juice
6 tablespoons finely chopped orange rind

Preheat the oven to 350 degrees. Cream the butter with 2 cups of sugar. Add the eggs and beat until light and fluffy. Sift 4½ cups of flour with the baking soda. Add the flour mixture, alternating with buttermilk, to the creamed mixture. Dust dates with remaining ¼ cup flour. Fold in the nuts and dates. Pour into 2 wax paper–lined or well greased and floured 4 by 8-inch loaf pans. Bake for 1 hour. Heat and stir the orange juice, orange rind, and remaining 1½ cups sugar until the sugar dissolves. Pour over the cakes after they have been removed from the oven. Let cool in the pans.

❖ *Yield: 16 serving*

Raisin Apple Coffee Cake

This recipe has its origins both in my Mom's recipes and in trial runs at various coffee roundtables. I love the way raisins and apples work so well together in this classic dessert.

"Alternating" pouring in the ingredients in this recipe—and in all of my recipes—helps you avoid lumps in your batter. It helps to gradually break the flour into the overall mix and blend it well. I learned the hard way about the importance of alternating when adding certain ingredients. When a recipe says *gradually* add something, it means *gradually.*

As for how to slice this particular coffee cake—not to mention all the others—it is a matter of first dividing it in half crosswise. Then you quarter both halves. And, voilà, the desired eight pieces.

4 tablespoons butter or margarine
1/4 cup plus 2 tablespoons sugar
1 egg
1 1/2 cups flour
2 teaspoons baking powder

1/2 teaspoon salt
1/2 cup milk
1/2 cup raisins
4 medium apples, thinly sliced
1 teaspoon cinnamon

Preheat the oven to 350 degrees. Cream the butter with ¼ cup of sugar. Blend in the egg. Sift together the flour, baking powder, and salt. Alternate adding the flour mix and milk to the creamed mixture. Fold the raisins into the batter. Pour into a 4 by 8-inch pan. Press the apple slices into the top of the batter. Sprinkle with cinnamon and 2 tablespoons of sugar. Bake for 35–40 minutes.

❖ *Yield: 8 servings*

There's no such thing as "too many" when it comes to apples!

Cookies and Pastries

Apple Bars

This is one of those fruity things that help one break away from all the sugary stuff. Granny Smith apples are again the best for this kind of recipe.

4 cups flour
1/2 teaspoon salt
2 cups sugar
1/2 pound (2 sticks) butter or margarine
5 cups chopped apples (using approximately 8 medium apples)

1 teaspoon cinnamon
1/4 teaspoon cardamom
1/2 teaspoon nutmeg
1/8 teaspoon ground cloves

Preheat the oven to 350 degrees. Sift together the flour, salt, and sugar. Cut the butter in to form cornmeal-sized crumbs. Reserve 1/2 cup of crumb mixture. Put half of the crumbs in a 13 by 9-inch pan. Press lightly. Bake for 10 minutes. Mix the apples with the reserved crumbs and toss with the cinnamon, cardamom, nutmeg, and cloves. Cover the baked crumb bottom with the apples and remaining crumb mixture. Bake for 35–40 minutes. Cool in pan and cut into squares.

❖ Yield: 8–12 servings

I save the peelings on the side for my apple nut and morning glory muffins.

Applesauce Squares

These squares really are more like cake in that they aren't as chewy as the other bars or squares. This is one of those recipes from when I first started baking. It was in my experimental "Suzy Homemaker" stage, meaning that it goes back at least thirty years—as old as my eldest daughter.

The use of quick oats here is important because they tend to blend better. The last topping suggestion, hot fudge, is something that really appeals to me, since fudge goes great with oats.

¼ teaspoon mace
1½ cups flour
1½ cups quick oats
¼ teaspoon salt

1 cup brown sugar
12 tablespoons (1½ sticks) butter
* or margarine*
1 quart unsweetened applesauce

Preheat the oven to 350 degrees. Combine all ingredients except applesauce. Mix to form coarse meal texture. Press half of the mixture into a 13 by 9 by 2-inch pan. Pour the applesauce over the crust. Top with the remaining half of the crumb mixture. Bake for 30–45 minutes. Serve warm with your favorite topping, such as ice cream, whipped cream, or hot fudge.

❖ *Yield: 8–12 servings*

Blueberry Upside-Down Squares

I have always loved blueberries, whether in muffins or in pies. In fact, about the only pie besides apple that I will eat is blueberry—I'm not a pie person. But I'm always looking for other ways to deal with blueberries besides in pie.

The fun and tricky thing about this recipe is that it involves flipping the cake over, bringing the blueberries you've placed on the bottom to the top. Once that is done, you have a complete item that you don't need to do anything else with, except maybe add a little whipped cream on top.

The trick to the flipping action begins with greasing the pan or lining it with paper and sprinkling it with flour. I personally like to use baker's parchment; it can be purchased on a roll, or you can get the bakery department of any big store to give you a few sheets of it. Wax paper is just fine, too.

As to the flipping, you have to do it quickly, while the cake is still hot. You can't let it sit for more than ten minutes after it has come out of the oven. Even with a paper-lined pan, you can't get away with letting the cake sit too much longer than ten minutes. If you wait too long, the cake will adhere to the pan, making it doubly difficult to get out.

Flipping it over is a messy art done with a twist of the wrist. Make sure you have a clear surface so that if you make any mistakes, you don't have cake falling off the table. Timing is everything with this recipe, as it is with pineapple upside-down cake. But the good news is that if you make the flip while it is still hot, you'll have a perfect dessert.

The orange zest can be obtained by using either a zester (really a fancy grater) or a vegetable peeler. Once you have the peel, you can use any knife to chop the rind finely. The peeler has an advantage over the grater because little bits of zest can get lost in a grater's holes.

1½ cups blueberries (fresh or frozen)
½ cup brown sugar, packed
1 tablespoon butter
¼ cup margarine
½ cup granulated sugar

1 egg, well beaten
1 teaspoon orange zest
1 cup flour
¼ teaspoon salt
1½ teaspoons baking powder
⅓ cup orange juice

Preheat the oven to 350 degrees. Simmer the blueberries, brown sugar, and butter in a saucepan for 5 minutes. Pour into a greased wax paper–lined 8 by 8 by 2-inch pan. Cream the margarine and sugar. Blend in the egg and orange zest. Sift the dry ingredients and add, alternating with the orange juice. Spoon the mixture over the berries, spreading it evenly. Bake for 40 minutes. Remove from oven and immediately flip pan over onto wax paper–lined surface. Carefully remove paper from cake. Serve warm with whipped cream.

❖ *Yield: 8–12 servings*

Quick Berry Pastry Squares

This recipe was given to me by a very dear friend I call "Cemetery Mary." I strolled into a cemetery in Hazleton, a town in northeastern Pennsylvania, and there she was with her two grandchildren. Now, cemeteries in this coal-mining part of the state are treated like parks. People are not intimidated by them. The other thing is that this was an all-white part of Pennsylvania, and she befriended me, something that really touched me. We had one very important thing in common: We both loved to bake.

As for this recipe, it involves a simple pie crust and working with confectioners' sugar. It is truly a quick and easy item to do, and all kinds of fruit can be incorporated in it, such as blueberries and strawberries.

For the pastry shell
2 cups flour
2 tablespoons sugar
½ pound (2 sticks) butter or
*   margarine*

For the filling
8 ounces cream cheese
1 cup confectioners' sugar
8 ounces prepared whipped cream
1 pint berries (such as raspberries,
*   blueberries, or strawberries)*
¼ cup granulated sugar
2 tablespoons cornstarch

Preheat the oven to 350 degrees. Combine the flour and sugar. Cut the butter into the mixture as for a pie crust. Press the mixture into a jelly roll pan or a 9 by 13 by 2-inch cake pan. Bake for 15 minutes. Cool for 10 minutes. To prepare the filling, whip the cream cheese. Gradually add the sugar, beating until light and fluffy. Fold in the prepared whipped cream. Spread this mixture on the crust. To make the filling, mix the berries with the sugar and the cornstarch and cook over low heat until the juice thickens. Cool for 10 minutes. Spread the filling on top of the cream cheese. Chill before serving.

Marti O'Connell gave me my wagon—I don't know if I could have made it without support like hers.

Cherry Cookies

These cookies celebrate George Washington. Now, as for the maraschino cherries, I just think of the decadence of chocolate-covered cherries and how wonderful they are on Valentine's Day. They are very sweet, really verging on being a candied item. But they are also soft. So sweet, so soft, so good—I mean, why not have a dessert built around them?

So cherry cookies were born. I was living at home, attending all those Tupperware parties, and I was always expected to come up with some new ideas. With this particular baked good, you wrap the dough around the cherries. You can do that more easily by dipping your fingers in some flour. These work equally well on Washington's Birthday, on Christmas, and for your sweetie on Valentine's Day.

2 tablespoons sugar
6 tablespoons confectioners' sugar
¼ pound (1 stick) butter or margarine

1 cup flour
30 maraschino cherries
1½ cups confectioners' sugar

Preheat the oven to 350 degrees. Mix together the sugars, butter, and flour. Drain the cherries, reserving the juice. Wrap a small amount of dough around each cherry and place on a baking sheet. Bake for 12–15 minutes. Mix the cherry juice with the confectioners' sugar. Drizzle over the warm cookies.

❖ *Yield: 2½ dozen*

Vegetables and Grains

There was a dichotomy running throughout my family's reaction to my choosing to become a professional baker. Initially, on hearing of my decision, my parents—especially my father—were staunchly opposed. My father basically saw me as more of a white-collar type. Especially in Washington, D.C., where so many of us were the direct descendants of slaves, we were trying to get away from stereotypical thinking. My family wanted to show that we had a higher level of ambition, that we had the desire to be successful and to achieve. To my father, the food industry was symbolic of slavery and subservience. That is what my grandmother and our ancesters in general did, and he didn't want me to go in that direction. They worried about how hard the industry would be on my body. The heat alone, up to 350 degrees coming from the industrial ovens, can certainly sap your energy. They felt I was an educated woman and didn't have to make a living this way.

But I'm nothing else if not a rebel. I persisted with my own ideas, my own plan, and my own way. I'm not necessarily a leader, and I'm not a follower per se, but I am an innovator.

All wrapped up and ready to go

I want to set a certain pace with a format that suits me. It certainly took many years for everyone to accept it, especially when in 1979 I left that very safe and comfortable corporate job with Blue Cross insurance to bake full time.

Domestically, I wanted my babies, and I enjoyed taking care of my house.

My Harriet Tubman look—directing my assistants outside the firehouse.

I wanted to be a real homemaker like June Cleaver. I wanted the American dream and, in a way, with a tall, handsome husband and beautiful children, I could be the perfect homemaker.

Because I had more than a semblance of control over my life, I never wanted anyone—starting with a husband—telling me what to do. I felt sure I wanted to be a businesswoman. That was my goal. I had told my husband to his face that I was going to do that and that nobody rules me.

Those first few months after I left the conventional workaday world were not easy ones. I was in considerable pain over my decision. At one point I actually began crying out to God to help me, so stark was my emotional pain. And you know what? Out of all the anguish, I really heard a still, quiet voice saying something like "I want you to bake." In that little one-bedroom apartment in Washington's Congress Heights district on Martin Luther King

Avenue, where I—a young divorcée—lived, that voice came to me and drove me to bake. Not just for friends and family, but professionally.

Soon I was reeling off my trusty carrot cake to make the $300 I used to buy my children their Christmas clothes. Then I took my cakes to the Adams Morgan section of Washington, first to a West African restaurant where my carrot cake made for a popular—if somewhat odd—dessert for an African meal. I went from pumping out one cake per day in my narrow kitchen to twenty cakes per day, one hundred cakes per week. Then came the bustling deli section of a very busy Washington liquor store as the next purveyor of cupcake versions of my winning carrot cake.

Once I was started on a roll, I built up a tremendous amount of self-confidence, thinking I could do anything and was invincible. Naturally, none of that proved exactly true. I remember going to one restaurant just near the White House, a really prestigious account. The manager became livid with me for making a cake delivery through the front door during the peak of his lunchtime business. His essential point was that I couldn't do business with him while he was doing business with others. I burst into tears when I left that place.

I was gaining success, but I was also learning some tough lessons. After absorbing those professional blows, I think I started telling my kids not to do what I'd done, not to follow in my footsteps. It really didn't seem worth it.

I think my children resented my lifestyle since it took so much time, and they didn't see a lot of money coming from it. We were always broke and poor. Baking ended up taking all my time and energy. But I think if I've taught my kids anything, it is to persevere and follow your instincts and personal beliefs, no matter what anybody else says. I think they've also learned from me that even if you don't always like or embrace what a person does, you should learn to accept it. My children accepted me and what I was doing without necessarily embracing it. I went totally against the grain.

When you raise essentially two generations of children, with a fifteen-year age span between the oldest and the youngest, you learn that being a mother demands giving individual attention to each child. As I learned the ropes of the baking business, I was learning how much I needed to accept my children for their individualism, and all I needed to worry about was laying the groundwork.

Now, despite all the trials of my baking world, my children surely know that I love them dearly and that they have always been primary for me. In a way, my baking business, such as it is, will be my main legacy to them, one that started with my mother. It is part of the legacy of being an independent woman and not being dependent on a man for anything.

At the end of the day, my personal bottom line is that for over twenty years my baking has lasted longer than my several marriages collectively. Baking has been the one constant in my life, the total of everything I've been about. Interestingly, by the time I had the desire to bake and saw my own business begin to develop, I was also married and a mother. I started to live by the saying "God bless the child that's got his own." I wanted to be self-enslaved, not a slave to someone else. It must have been then that I discovered I had to develop perseverance to attain my dream of being a baker.

Ironically, as I was developing this perseverance, my parents were coming around to my way of thinking. Because I've made my way in a kind of entrepreneurial venture, my father has grudgingly admired what I've done.

My newfound drive and
determination must have reminded
my father of his mother, who had brought
thirteen children into the world and
had an industrious husband who was
the son of a slave. His wife never had
to work for any white folks, while
my mother's mother did. Both women
struggled to survive; they had kids to care
for and did everything by the book.

*Left to right: My sister Olga, me, my
father, Lenzie, and my sister Brenda.
My father still wears that bow tie.*

I really feel I attained my business
success, such as it is, through being a living merger of my two families.
On one side, I had a grandfather who built houses and a grandmother who
helped maintain several households. My father's father put down the
foundation—literally—for an empire to grow. Now my father runs his father's
business. The work ethic and persistence comes from both sides.

Even if my mother at first objected to my not pursuing a more
"respectable" profession, be it lawyering or doctoring, she always called me a
trooper. She firmly believed in what I was about, no matter what anybody else
said. Part of her supported me very strongly in what I did. She understood I
was taking a different avenue. I learned a lot simply by watching her. She
worked very hard at her craft, and I was just striving to equal her excellence—
and not just hers, but all the other women in my extended family, who
became my teachers by extension. I wanted to learn what had made them so
great. I wanted to be great just like them, to equal their excellence.

In our classically raised family, the daughters were always the mother's

The alchemist at work—pouring yeast

responsibility. My mother wanted me to finish college, and I'm sure that when I didn't, part of her felt I had wasted the money. Instead I went off to have babies. But to the end my mother firmly supported everything I did. All I had to do was remember that although her husband—my father—didn't want her working, she had insisted on having her own life and career. And, like her, I didn't listen to anybody else, either, when it came to mapping out what I wanted to do.

As long as I was independent, pursuing my baking, my mother always gave me ideas, suggestions, and new ways to do things. I'll never forget that no sooner was I married to my first husband and tending my own home for the first time than I called my mother and asked for advice on what to serve my husband for dinner. I wasn't prepared to cook for a man—especially one who had grown up with *his* grandmother, a woman who used to be the private cook for the head of the whole Marriott Corporation. But if this was a challenge, I figured I would rise above it as well. And all in all, my mother was always behind me and never discouraged me.

I remember at one point my mother told me that I should purposely never learn how to type, because if I did, I might find myself stuck behind a typewriter for the rest of my life. What she meant was that none of my other skills or passions—that is, my baking—would ever come through if I settled for second best.

....

Although I thought I had found my place as both a young wife and mother, I was truly a bit rudderless. Both a practical and, frankly, a spiritual direction were missing from my life. It was only as I started to bake on a serious basis that I discovered just how spiritual, near religious, an experience it can be, this creating something out of nothing.

They say that God created man from dirt. In the creation scheme of things, the final result doesn't make *us* look like dirt. Flour is like that same handful of dirt. In baking, the same magical processes happen. The humblest ingredients come together in such a way that their original form all but disappears. You take flour, sugar, eggs, and butter, and when you end up with a loaf of bread, you don't see any of that flour or sugar in a single slice. In other cooking, you might put the best sauce in the world on top of a piece of meat, but when you slice that new creation, it's still the same meat it always was. It hasn't changed.

For me, the transformation that takes place in baking elevates it from the role of a mere culinary act. Baking has always been therapeutic for me. Baking sprang from a very tough time in my life, and it acted as a kind of panacea for contending with the turmoil around me.

There are rules and a structure to baking. For a person like myself, who lives a rather free life, knowing that bread might not rise or a cake might fall—in essence, knowing that I will pay if I violate the structure or break the rules—was a good thing. That structure brought me into focus. I had to concentrate completely on what I was doing in the kitchen—even if it meant polishing my rusty high school math and chemistry skills. But in the end, baking became just so gratifying, so much better than going to a bar and grabbing a drink.

Frankly, I think everybody should do something with their hands. Working with my hands when I bake, I'm not using any machinery, so whatever I'm putting together is something that generates from me. It then becomes the kind of spiritual experience where it is my spirit that is really doing the job. When I bake, I obviously touch whatever I do. And that touch is passed on to whoever eats what I create. That means they receive the passion I put into it.

Waving to another satisfied customer

Muffins

Carrot Muffins

I originally began baking a carrot cake when I started catering commercially instead of just baking for friends and family. And the easy offshoot of that cake was the carrot muffin. In fact, from my baked carrot cake, both muffins and a cupcake were born. My mother ate a lot of carrot sticks when she was pregnant with me. She told me much later how she wasn't surprised that I ended up creating a carrot cake. Perhaps carrots were ordained to be a big part of my baking well before I was born.

As for these muffins, there is no real dairy product in them. And did I say healthy? These carrot muffins are chock-full of that essential carotin. It's a great way for your body to stock up, especially if you are not partial to raw carrots.

The secret of this carrot muffin is the mace. It is an incredible spice. My carrot cake is the one that brought me into the large-scale baking business to begin with, and this carrot muffin is just a continuation of it. I believe in dancing with the one who brought you. Any collection of my recipes has to have a carrot cake on board.

Be sure that you sift the dry ingredients. If you don't, they have a tendency to lump together, especially the flour. Not sifting will make an inconsistent batter, with too much salt in one corner and too much of

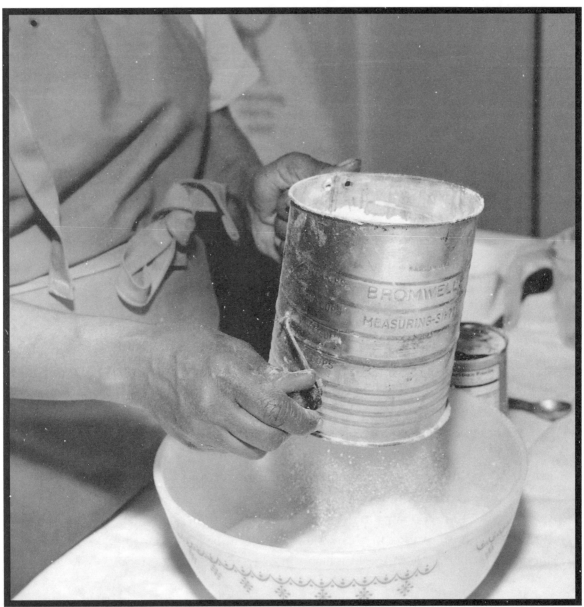

Sifting—it's worth the extra time and effort.

something else in another. Sifting guarantees that it is balanced and homogeneous. Sifting breaks everything down so it will then blend together. If you don't have a real sifter, which is really a fancy strainer, run a fork through the dry ingredients.

4 medium-size carrots, grated with peel
1 cup oil
1 cup sugar
2 eggs
2 cups flour

2 teaspoons baking powder
1 teaspoon baking soda
1 teaspoon salt
½ teaspoon cinnamon
½ teaspoon nutmeg
¼ teaspoon mace

Preheat the oven to 350 degrees. Using the medium speed on a mixer, combine the carrots, oil, and sugar. Add the eggs one at a time. Sift the dry ingredients and gradually add them to the carrot batter. Spoon the batter into a wax paper–lined 12-unit muffin pan. Bake for 25–30 minutes.

❖ *Yield: twelve 2–4-ounce muffins or six 6–8-ounce muffins*

Corn Muffins

These corn muffins are a direct descendant of my experience with cornbread, one of the first things I ever learned to bake from scratch. The transition was pretty easy.

The purpose of the hot oil is to tighten up the grain of the cornmeal. Any hot item combined with flour or a grain product will make it more dense. The hot oil acts as a binder for the cornmeal, eliminating that crumbling factor and making it more adhesive and homogeneous. Of course, in the original family corn muffin recipe, that binder would be bacon drippings or margarine, but hot vegetable oil seems more healthful.

Making the corn muffin meant extending my love of cornbread. Cornbread is something I must have whenever I have fish. My family's Friday supper ritual was cornbread with shad, rockfish, or bass. It's really an African-American tradition to combine cornbread with fish (and that's usually fish fried in lard), some of the best-tasting food in the world. My comfort with cornmeal and, thus, corn muffins probably dates back to my Indian blood on both sides of my family, especially to my great-grandmother on my father's side, which has some North Carolina Cherokee ancestors.

4 tablespoons butter or margarine
¼ cup oil
2 cups cornmeal
1 cup flour
½ cup sugar

1 tablespoon baking powder
1 teaspoon salt
2 eggs
1 cup milk

Preheat the oven to 350 degrees. Melt the butter and oil together. Combine all the dry ingredients. Make a well in the center. Add the eggs, milk, and hot butter and oil. Blend together before spooning into a wax paper–lined 12-unit muffin pan. Bake for 20–25 minutes.

❖ *Yield: twelve 2–4-ounce muffins or six 6–8-ounce muffins*

Oat Bran Muffins

There I was, off on one of my periodic health kicks, when I came up with an oat bran muffin. I had been hearing from customers and friends about the need for a muffin with healthy whole-grain flour rather than processed flour. Oat bran muffins seemed like a good idea.

It took a little bit of trial and error: When I first started baking them, they tended to sag and sink in the middle. I had put too much liquid in them. I also discovered an old saying when trying to develop the right temperature and length of time to cook these muffins: You can't rush anything. Baking is about patience. There is a lot of waiting in baking, especially when you are experimenting, as I was with this oat bran muffin. It's not about hurrying and turning up the heat. You can't do that in baking. Baking involves a lot of standing around time, which is the bad news.

The good news is that you can do a lot of other things while you are waiting. You can start to clean up the mess you've made in the kitchen. Also, you can plan where you are going to place the hot pan when you remove it from the oven. You should always know in advance where that hot pan will go before you have to start balancing it in your hands.

You should also never let your oven go bare. This means that while something is baking, a new project can be started, and as soon as the first item comes out of the oven, the new one can be slipped right in after it. This is especially true at holiday time when most people have the toughest time organizing how to use their oven in the most efficient way because they are baking so many different things.

I discovered that for the perfect oat bran muffin, the best thing to do is let it sit, which allows the grain to absorb the liquid. This is where the waiting and the patience of baking comes in. Don't count on the heat of the oven to make all that absorption happen. The sinking of the muffin's middle stopped when I allowed the oats to do a lot of the absorbing. I mean, oats are very absorbent on their own. If you leave raw oats in water for a while, you will have oatmeal. It may not be hot oatmeal, but the oats will absorb enough of the liquid to become soft.

This oat bran muffin, which formerly had a sinking middle, makes the baker focus on its center. The heat from the oven is going from the outside in, and once it gets inside, that is when whatever rising you want to occur will happen. But the key with this and all other muffins and other baking is giving the muffin time for the chemical reactions to take place. If you have to rush this or any other muffin, don't bother with it. Come back and do it another day.

2 cups old-fashioned or rolled oats
½ cup flour
¾ cup brown sugar
1 teaspoon baking powder
1 teaspoon baking soda
¼ teaspoon mace

4 tablespoons butter or margarine,
*   melted*
¼ cup oil
¾ cup milk
2 eggs

Preheat the oven to 350 degrees. Combine all the dry ingredients. Make a well in the center. Add the butter, oil, milk, and eggs. Let the batter set for 5–10 minutes. Spoon the batter into a wax paper–lined 12-unit muffin pan. Bake for 30 minutes.

Variation: Add ½ cup raisins, ½ cup nuts, or ½ cup chocolate chips.

❖ *Yield: twelve 2–4-ounce muffins or six 6–8-ounce muffins*

Tomato Soup Muffins

This was a recipe from my sister-in-law. She's a stupendous cook, and one day when she brought a tomato soup cake, I knew that if I made certain adjustments to it, it would come out as a very interesting and tasty muffin.

In terms of moving ingredients around from cake to muffin, I had to increase and decrease certain dry products and decrease the liquid content of the cake. In the end, the tomato soup muffin has a sweet tomato flavor without any hint of saltiness.

Of course the tomato soup should be just plain tomato, with no rice or other ingredients. It has all the flavorings of a spice cake and a deep, red velvet color.

1 can (11 ounces) tomato soup	1 teaspoon baking soda
1/4 cup oil	2 teaspoons baking powder
4 tablespoons butter or margarine, melted	2 eggs
1 cup sugar	1 cup raisins
2 cups flour	1 teaspoon cinnamon
	1/4 teaspoon ground basil

Preheat the oven to 350 degrees. Mix together the soup, oil, butter, and sugar. Sift together the flour, baking soda, and baking powder. Add the eggs one at a time to the soup mix. Gradually add the flour mix. Fold in the raisins, cinnamon, and basil. Spoon into a 12-unit muffin pan. Bake for 25–30 minutes.

❖ *Yield: twelve 2–4-ounce muffins or six 6–8-ounce muffins*

Pumpkin Muffins

These will always remind me of Halloween back in Rochester, New York. After the season was over, the question was always what to do with the rest of that carved pumpkin. As a baker, you always want to use every bit of an ingredient you have.

I proceeded to break the pumpkin down and carve out the meat, getting rid of the seeds. First, I started out with fresh pumpkin pies, adapting an old recipe for sweet potato pie. Then I wondered if I couldn't shift that pumpkin pie recipe into a pumpkin bread loaf. From that loaf the muffins eventually emerged.

The pumpkin loaf itself was very heavy, with a lot of pumpkin baked right in its center. It took on the consistency of a cobbler, with the pumpkin all but falling right into its middle, surrounded by a very soft crust.

The actual transition from the pumpkin loaf to the muffin made me think more about how the pumpkin worked in a pie, surrounded by the flour of the pie crust. I needed to know how pumpkin meat reacted when flour was incorporated. The pumpkin loaf became a test for the muffin. What I discovered is that since pumpkin is extremely watery—even in canned form— I needed less pumpkin and more flour to absorb the excess pumpkin liquid.

Cardamom is a nice touch for this recipe. It helps bring out the pumpkin's flavor. Like mace, only a pinch is needed, and at $54 per pound, you want to use just a pinch.

The pumpkin muffin itself is a great Thanksgiving addition, since fresh pumpkin is available only from early October through the first week or two of

December. Cooking the pumpkin down, like cooking squash, involves dealing with its fibrous, sinewy insides. A food processor allows you to leave the fiber in. The resulting muffin comes out a nice yellow squashlike color.

I really am an autumnal person in that I've always loved the colors of fall, especially the reds, oranges, yellows, and earth tones. Although my mother died in autumn, I still prefer this season to any other.

½ cup pumpkin	*½ teaspoon cinnamon*
1 cup oil	*½ teaspoon nutmeg*
1 cup brown sugar	*¼ teaspoon mace*
2 cups flour	*¼ teaspoon cardamom*
2 teaspoons baking powder	*2 eggs*
1 teaspoon baking soda	*¼ cup slivered almonds (optional)*
1 teaspoon salt	

Preheat the oven to 350 degrees. Blend the pumpkin, oil, and sugar with an electric mixer at medium speed. Sift together all the dry ingredients including the spices. Add the eggs one at a time to the pumpkin mix. Gradually add the sifted ingredients. Spoon the batter into a wax paper–lined 12-unit muffin pan. Sprinkle the tops with toasted almonds if desired. Bake for 25–30 minutes.

❖ *Yield: twelve 2–4-ounce muffins or six 6–8-ounce muffins*

Raisin Bran Muffins

I definitely thought about the breakfast cereal when I came up with this twist on the standard oat bran muffin.

While I was doing my little walkathons with my wagon, everyone would request some kind of bran muffin. In the same breath, they also asked for fat-free.

Although I firmly believe the public truly enjoys the taste of fat, cholesterol, and sugar, I accepted their requests for these low-fat, bran muffins. I chose not to use the premade commercial cereal but rather the whole bran. The purpose was to arrive as close to natural as I could. Those on a health kick don't want the many additives that are in the premade cereal.

But what one finds out when making a muffin like the raisin bran one is that no matter how much a consumer says he or she wants the healthier ingredients, at the end of the day they are still quietly seeking the cholesterol, fat, and sugar.

A great day to be out selling muffins

2 cups 100% whole bran
1/2 cup flour
3/4 cup brown sugar
1 teaspoon baking soda
1 teaspoon baking powder
1/4 teaspoon mace

2 eggs
1/4 cup oil
4 tablespoons butter or margarine
3/4 cup milk
1/2 cup raisins

Preheat the oven to 350 degrees. Mix together by hand the bran, flour, sugar, baking soda, baking powder, and mace. Make a well in the center. Add the eggs, oil, butter, and milk. Mix by hand. Fold in the raisins. Spoon the batter into a wax paper–lined 12-unit muffin pan and bake for 25–30 minutes.

❖ *Yield: twelve 2–4-ounce muffins or six 6–8-ounce muffins*

Quick Breads

Oatmeal Loaf

Nearly every morning my mother would make us oatmeal—without fail, like the sun rising every day—until I was around eight years old.

I have read a fair amount of Dickens (it was required reading when I was growing up), so I know that oatmeal is nothing more than gruel. I call it as I see it. It has no real flavor, and you either like it or you don't.

As for the icing, it is coconut, and along with the nuts, it gives flavor to the oatmeal.

The evaporated milk is a real throwback to the Depression when people couldn't afford whole milk. Evaporated milk is useful here because it thickens the icing.

Who didn't grow up with evaporated milk?

For the loaf

1¼ cups boiling water
1 cup old-fashioned oats
¼ pound (1 stick) butter or
*   margarine*
1 cup white sugar
1 cup brown sugar
2 eggs
1 teaspoon baking soda
1½ cups flour
¼ teaspoon mace
¼ teaspoon salt

For the icing

¼ pound (1 stick) butter or
*   margarine*
¼ cup evaporated milk
¾ cup brown sugar
½ teaspoon vanilla extract
1 cup coconut, flaked
1 cup chopped nuts

Preheat the oven to 350 degrees. Combine the boiling water, oats, and butter. Let stand for 20 minutes. Add the remaining ingredients and mix well by hand. Pour into a wax paper–lined 16 by 8-inch loaf pan or two 4 by 8-inch loaf pans. Bake for 35–40 minutes.

To make the icing: Bring all the ingredients to a boil in a small saucepan. Remove from heat and beat slightly. Pour over the warm cake. Place under the broiler for 5 minutes.

❖ *Yield: 8–12 servings*

Pumpkin Loaf

This brings back memories of Halloweens spent up in the northern reaches of New York State. Like everyone else, we would always have this big old pumpkin, carved up into a jack-o'-lantern. And after the holiday was over, it seemed a real waste to take this pumpkin and throw it out. Then it hit me like a bolt of lightning. Since we were through with the pumpkin, I grabbed one of those big French chef's knives we had—a really sharp one—and started cutting the pumpkin. I cut it into big sections and put it, skin and all, into a big stockpot. Once the pumpkin was well cooked, the meat began to turn a light, clear yellow. I took a regular spoon and started scraping the meat off the skin. It came off easily.

At this point you do encounter a problem with the pumpkin's fibrous, sinewy texture. Use a food processor to break up any fibers that still linger and to blend the soaked-up water with the pumpkin meat.

The seeds are another matter. Once they are scraped away, you can rinse and salt them, and bake them on a cookie sheet. They make great snacks.

2 cups pumpkin, preferably fresh
1½ cups sugar
1 cup oil
3 eggs
2 cups flour
2 teaspoons baking powder

1 teaspoon baking soda
1 teaspoon salt
½ teaspoon cinnamon
½ teaspoon nutmeg
½ teaspoon mace
¼ teaspoon cardamom

Preheat the oven to 350 degrees. Cream the pumpkin, sugar, and oil. Add the eggs. Sift together all the dry ingredients including the spices. Gradually add to the creamed pumpkin. Bake in a 4 by 8-inch loaf pan for 45 minutes to 1 hour, or until the center is dense and moist.

❖ *Yield: 8–12 servings*

Rhubarb Loaf

Personally, all I had really been familiar with in the rhubarb family was strawberry rhubarb pie. I had never really heard of just rhubarb pie until I moved to northern New York State. Rhubarb is, literally, quite a wild thing. It is leafy, with a colorful red stem, and it grows everywhere, starting with your backyard.

¼ pound (1 stick) butter
* or margarine*
1½ cups brown sugar
1 teaspoon vanilla extract
1 egg, beaten
1 cup buttermilk

1 teaspoon baking soda
2 cups flour
1½ cups chopped raw rhubarb
½ cup white sugar
1 teaspoon cinnamon

Preheat the oven to 350 degrees. Cream the butter and brown sugar. Blend in the vanilla, egg, and buttermilk. Sift together the baking soda and flour. Add the rhubarb and stir. Pour into a wax paper–lined 9 by 13-inch cake pan. Combine the white sugar and cinnamon, and sprinkle over the batter. Bake for 45 minutes to 1 hour.

❖ *Yield: 8–12 servings*

Zucchini Bread

I personally like zucchini a lot. It has always been one of my favorites, though it doesn't have much flavor on its own. Like the pumpkin, zucchini is part of the squash family, and this type of vegetable needs to be worked with raw—not cooked—because it is already too mushy at that stage. You certainly don't want anything that even approaches overripe, especially since you'll be working with the peel, the very thing many people throw away but should be eating.

2 cups grated zucchini
1 cup oil
2 eggs
1 cup sugar
2 cups flour
2 teaspoons baking powder

1 teaspoon baking soda
1 teaspoon salt
⅛ teaspoon cardomom
¼ teaspoon mace
½ cup chopped toasted almonds

Preheat the oven to 350 degrees. Combine the zucchini, oil, eggs, and sugar. Sift together the dry ingredients and gradually add them to the zucchini mix. Blend in the nuts. Bake in a 4 by 8-inch loaf pan for 45 minutes.

❖ *Yield: 8–12 servings*

Carrot Cupcakes

This is another secret recipe I'm giving away. This is the one that a lot—I mean *a lot*—of people have tried to wrest from me. I remember my mother, who saw how well these were selling, kept on telling me: "Now, Linda, don't you give that recipe away. If you do, you will be giving all your money away." Well, I think the world can have it now!

What makes it work? The orange marmalade is certainly a big factor. And the pineapple, coconut, and walnuts. But I think the real secret is the mace.

Another secret is that the batter can be made in advance, and it can be refrigerated or frozen. The finished cupcakes themselves can also be frozen after being baked. For some reason, after freezing, they end up with a better flavor.

2 cups grated carrots
1½ cups sugar
1 cup oil
3 eggs
2 cups flour
2 teaspoons baking powder
1 teaspoon baking soda
1 teaspoon salt

½ teaspoon cinnamon
½ teaspoon nutmeg
¼ teaspoon mace
2 tablespoons orange marmalade
2 tablespoons crushed pineapple
½ cup chopped walnuts
4 tablespoons flaked coconut

Preheat the oven to 350 degrees. Combine the carrots, sugar, oil, and eggs. Sift together the flour, baking powder, soda, salt, and spices. Gradually add to the carrot mixture. Fold in the marmalade, pineapple, nuts, and coconut. Spoon into a wax paper–lined 12-unit muffin pan. Bake for 30–35 minutes. Ice with your favorite icing (see recipe for My Favorite Frosting, page 174).

❖ *Yield: twelve 6-ounce cupcakes*

Zucchini Chocolate Cake

I got this recipe from my stay in northeastern Pennsylvania. That summer of 1987 was my first real exposure to what I'd call "real America." There, the cooking leans more toward German and Italian influences, with lots of fruits and vegetables and, thus, heavier cakes.

This particular cake is very moist, and you wouldn't even know it has zucchini in it unless you were told.

4 tablespoons margarine
4 tablespoons butter
1/2 cup oil
1 1/2 cups sugar
2 cups shredded zucchini
1 egg

1 teaspoon vanilla extract
2 1/2 cups flour
4 tablespoons unsweetened cocoa
2 teaspoons baking soda
1/2 cup buttermilk
2 cups (12 ounces) chocolate chips

Preheat the oven to 350 degrees. Cream together the margarine, butter, oil, and sugar. Add the zucchini, egg, and vanilla. Sift together the flour, cocoa, and baking soda. Add the flour mixture and buttermilk alternately to the creamed mixture. Pour into a 10-inch round tube pan and sprinkle the top of the batter with chocolate chips. Bake for 45–50 minutes.

❖ *Yield: 15 servings*

Cookies and Pastries

Cornflake Cookies

This is one of the recipes my mom gave me, and it stuck. Cornflakes are just another grain, and it makes these cookies crunchy while also adding chewiness. The coconut, which I love to use, adds a nice flavor.

2 cups flour
1 teaspoon baking soda
1/2 teaspoon salt
1/2 teaspoon baking powder
20 tablespoons (2 1/2 sticks) butter
    or margarine

1 cup white sugar
1 cup brown sugar, packed
2 eggs, beaten
1 teaspoon vanilla extract
2 cups flaked coconut
2 cups cornflakes

Preheat the oven to 350 degrees. Sift together the flour, baking soda, salt, and baking powder. Cream the butter, gradually adding the white and brown sugars. Beat until light and fluffy. Add the eggs and vanilla. Blend the dry ingredients into the creamed mixture. Mix in the coconut and cornflakes. Drop by teaspoonful onto a greased or wax paper–lined cookie sheet.

Bake for 8–10 minutes.

❖ Yield: 8 dozen

Oat Bran Brownies

Unlike a fair number of the other recipes that have the stamp of my mother on them, this one is 100 percent me.

The cocoa and oil create a chocolate paste, and the final product looks as if you just melted a block of chocolate. Real chocolate is hard to store because it is quite sensitive to changes in air temperature and humidity. So the best way is to start out with dry cocoa and add oil to it by hand.

3 cups old-fashioned or rolled oats
1 cup flour
1 cup brown sugar
½ cup white sugar
¼ teaspoon baking soda
¼ teaspoon mace
½ pound (2 sticks) butter or
* margarine*

2 eggs
6 tablespoons unsweetened cocoa
3 tablespoons oil
1 cup raisins
1 cup (6 ounces) chocolate chips

Preheat the oven to 350 degrees. Combine the oats, flour, brown sugar, white sugar, baking soda, and mace. Cut the butter into pieces and add to the oat mixture (as in making a pie crust). Make a well in the center. Blend in the eggs by hand. Mix the cocoa and oil to form a paste. Fold the raisins, chocolate chips, and cocoa paste into the dough, making sure not to overmix. Spoon the mixture into a 9 by 13-inch pan and spread with a spatula. Bake for 30 minutes. Let cool for 10 minutes. Frost with fudge icing (recipe follows).

❖ *Yield: 8–12 servings*

Fudge Icing

¼ pound (1 stick) butter
or margarine
6 tablespoons unsweetened
cocoa

4 tablespoons evaporated milk
1 teaspoon vanilla extract
1 pound confectioners' sugar

Place the butter, cocoa, evaporated milk, and vanilla in a small saucepan and bring to a boil. Remove from the heat and stir in the sugar. Spread over the brownies.

Oatmeal Drop Cookies

U nfortunately, more often than not you grow up getting really poor oatmeal cookies that come from the grocery store or in school lunches. The "real deal"—the homemade ones—are chewy with nuts and great flavor. The flavor of home-baked oatmeal cookies is totally different from the prefab, stamped-out-by-a-machine ones. My mom made the original oatmeal cookies a couple of times, and it really left an impression on me.

Overall, the recipe is an easy one. A working mom can do it on a weekend as a fun project. It's amazing how many working moms do things like that even though their lives are really, really busy.

2 cups sugar
½ cup milk
3 tablespoons unsweetened cocoa
4 tablespoons butter or margarine

½ cup peanut butter
3 cups oatmeal
1 teaspoon vanilla extract

Boil the sugar, milk, cocoa, and butter for 3 minutes. Remove from the heat and add the peanut butter, oatmeal, and vanilla. Drop on wax paper. Let cool and eat.

❖ *Yield: 4–6 dozen*

Confections

As I look forward, I am always aware of looking backward. Gazing at the yellowed pieces of paper that contain my recipes, my family's recipes, I find a fragileness and yet a strength in them. They remind me that the person who religiously followed those recipes was not the baker she is today.

Saying good-bye at the jewelry shop

Looking ahead, I don't forget that my mother passed these recipes along to me thirty years ago. They represent, in some sense, thirty years of my life. When I look at them, so many things rush forward. I remember my first marriage, when these recipes helped me start keeping house. I remember with real clarity my mother's three main cookbooks, all from the Church of the Atonement bazaar.

The best parts of my baking life—my most reliable recipes—came from those books. They were designed by people who really cared about what they were doing. They were housewives and homemakers who gave their families the best of everything—and their recipes were always accurate, down to crossing the last *t*.

The picture on the left is my mother at Penn State, where she got her master's degree. On the right is her graduation picture from North Carolina College in 1937.

When I look down the road at my forty-eight years, I think about the contrast between the rock-solid reliability of those books and the casualness of commercial recipes. Over time, I've done my share of investing in some major cookbooks, and in nearly all of these fancy books there is a requirement for the home baker that is difficult to fulfill. How often does the average baker keep cake flour at home? People might have Bisquick, but cake flour? But with the old recipes and the ones I use, those who bake on a somewhat regular basis will end up using what they normally keep in their kitchen.

Looking into my crystal ball, I see myself working as a baker not in a commercial kitchen but at home, using my home kitchen as a laboratory for innovative baking. Naturally, I would want my recipes to continue to be generated by someone in a commercial kitchen, but baking at home would allow me to create other desserts, which takes time. So many of my earliest ideas were created out of necessity. Now it might be nice to stretch out and explore. As I delegate more and more of my baking work to others, I hope I can pass along baking as a reasonable career choice to those who might be aimless, searching for something meaningful to do.

When someone like my best girlfriend's daughter shows an interest in what I'm doing and, more to the point, is willing to wake up at four in the morning to help me, then it hits me like a bolt of lightning: This person is dead serious about baking, and her innate ability should be cultivated. She helps out so much that now when she makes the finished muffin, nobody realizes there has been a switch and a new muffin lady is in training. All of seventeen, she is coming up with new ideas on her own. She will say, "Listen, Miss Linda, I think we should do this much today," and when her suggestion carries more weight than my attitude, we go with her way. She also works on her own independent ideas. She'll take scraps of dough, load them up with nuts and brown sugar syrup, and lavish some kind of heavy icing on them. She has spun this out, and with a name like Melissa's Nutty Buddy, she can probably get $1.75 for each one. I really enjoy giving her the license to do that, to experiment at my expense. Maybe I could, by example, play a role in bringing back the apprentice system.

The problem with today's students is that not only are they not learning the basics, but when they do learn something, it usually leads to a mastery of only one thing. If per chance one of the key ingredients is missing in the kitchen, these students won't know what to do next. Instead of applying plain old common sense, they panic.

The moment of truth

I've raised four children, and I know that while it would be tempting to start my future students as early as eight years old, the attention span of an eight-year-old is not the same as that of a thirteen-year old. By ages sixteen and seventeen, they are starting to shape their thoughts of a career.

My youngest child might be the only one to receive fully my cooking inheritance, since my other kids really don't like to cook. They have never stood around the kitchen watching me do what I do, as I did with my mother.

Oliver is my youngest at age fourteen.

I understand their attitude. They wanted to go to college and I didn't want to, though I went to make my parents happy.

I hope that in the future I will still have my fire burning inside. I think it will be a steady blaze, as opposed to the raging, out-of-control inferno it can be.

My inner combustion does need to calm down a little bit, but I don't think I will ever lose that fire in the belly.

I'd like to encourage people to step out there and live, accepting that if they fall, they can pick themselves up and continue to walk the line until they get to where they want to go.

I want to push people away from being anesthetized and too comfortable in their complacency. If they reach that point, they might as well dig themselves the six-foot hole and pull the dirt in on top of them. Life will always be about growing and expanding, and that is how I want to continue to live it. To do, not to talk. To be open to new ideas, whether they are suggestions coming from a child or a much older person. I need to remind myself that I learned to be creative and entrepreneurial while still trying to figure out how to make a living. Back when I was struggling and couldn't afford one hundred pounds of flour or fifty pounds of sugar, I could still buy myself five pounds of flour and one pound of sugar, and a stick or two of margarine. I worked those ingredients to see what might happen.

The future looks rosy to me. I think I'm finally coming full circle after twenty years. I'd like to see "the Muffin Lady" shine from coast to coast. With my "Muffin Lady" places, there would be cakes, pies, breads, and muffins. We would cover every aspect of what the traditional bakery used to provide. It's sad that the corner bakery doesn't exist anymore—maybe because the old neighborhood has disappeared. It's now at the mall.

I admit that it's been a long road to here, yet it hasn't always been a struggle. God has been very good to me. Even when the struggles were going on, they never really lasted that long. I pulled my Radio Flyer wagon for less than a year. That struggle ended quickly. Mine is very much a "this, too, shall pass" approach. My mother always used to remind me of that. I'm only sorry she is not able to share all of this with me now.

I truly believe she is smiling down on me. I think she sees

New wheels someone just gave me—a kindness I've never forgotten.

how blessed I am with my four beautiful children. But you know what I think I carry most of all from my mother and my field? Their aroma. I've been told many times that I smell of sugar, that I have the smell of baking around me. It fills my clothes, my hair, and my skin. People always pick up that faint scent of vanilla. It just seems to linger long after I've put the mixing bowl away. Personally, I don't smell it, but there must be something to it.

I hope I won't lose that aura around me. I'm highly complimented by it. If I continue to smell like baked bread or anything with sugar in it, that would be fine with me.

Muffins

Apple Crumb Nut Muffins

The "diced" apples for the apple crumb nut offer a happy medium between slicing large chunks of the fruit into the dessert and using the fine shavings of "grated" apples.

As for the streusel topping, this is one of a few recipes where using your hands to create it will make all the difference in the world. The danger in using a mixer to combine the streusel ingredients is that the end result might be other than a streusel topping. It risks becoming more like a dough. You don't want the topping's ingredients to become so blended together that they bind. Rather, they should stay loose. Once it becomes like dough, you have quite another product on your hands.

A brief word on working with one's hands: If you can't put your

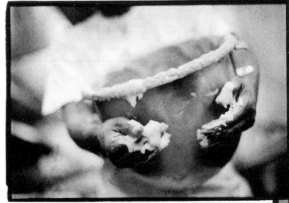

Only your hands can tell you if the batter needs more flour to tighten it up.

hands in it, you had better not do it at all. Working with food is messy by nature. If you have a problem with the mess, you'd better not be involved in baking. Every baker has a touch and needs to pass on a certain spirituality of that touch to the creation. This means putting your hands in and on it. However much baking is a science—and it is one—if you don't have that touch, you won't make it. If I really knew what that touch was, I would bottle it and sell it, making a real fortune.

2 medium-to-large-size apples
2 cups flour
1 cup sugar
1 tablespoon baking powder
1 teaspoon salt
2 eggs

¾ cup milk
4 tablespoons butter or margarine,
*   melted*
1 teaspoon vanilla extract
¼ cup oil

Preheat the oven to 350 degrees. Core and dice the apples. Sift together the dry ingredients. Make a well in the center. Blend in the eggs, milk, butter, vanilla, and oil. Fold in the apples. Spoon the batter into a wax paper–lined 12-unit muffin pan. Top with streusel topping (recipe follows). Bake for 30–35 minutes.

❖ *Yield: twelve 2–4-ounce muffins or six 6–8-ounce muffins*

Streusel Topping

1 cup brown sugar
1 cup white sugar
1 teaspoon cinnamon
1 teaspoon nutmeg
⅛ teaspoon ground cloves

¼ cup flour
¼ pound (1 stick) butter or
  margarine
½ cup chopped walnuts

Mix all the dry ingredients except the nuts. Cut the butter into the mix, using your hands to break into large chunks. Mix by hand until small balls form. Toss the nuts lightly into the mix.

Making streusel topping by breaking the butter into pieces.

Burnt Sugar Muffins

This originates from a burnt sugar cake, which suggests that almost any cake recipe can be turned into a muffin recipe. Burnt sugar really looks like molasses. Beware: You have to burn a lot of sugar to get the amount you need. You may need only a teaspoon of the final product, but you have to burn a cup of sugar to get it.

Now, burning sugar can be dangerous. It is highly flammable: If you burn it too long, it will catch fire. When you pour out the liquefied sugar, make sure you put it in a heat-resistant container. I once used a glass bottle, and it broke on me. While you are cooking sugar in a saucepan, watch it constantly. And certainly don't burn yourself. Nothing burns you like hot sugar since it must reach a very high temperature. Anyone who has ever baked will attest to the fact that when it burns, it hurts.

What you get after you've burned the sugar is a wonderful flavoring that adds moisture to the cake. It also serves as a natural preservative and helps increase the cake's shelf life.

1¾ cups sugar
¼ pound (1 stick) butter or
   margarine
2 egg yolks, beaten
2 cups flour

3 teaspoons baking powder
¾ cup milk
3 teaspoons burnt sugar
2 egg whites, beaten until stiff
⅛ teaspoon mace

To make 3 teaspoons of burnt sugar: Burn 1 cup sugar in a saucepan over medium-low to low heat until it has turned to a dark brown liquid. Add ½ cup hot water. Stir and boil for 1 minute.

Preheat the oven to 350 degrees. Cream the sugar and butter. Add the egg yolks. Sift the flour and baking powder together, and mix in alternately with the milk. Add the burnt sugar and fold in the egg whites and mace. Spoon into a wax paper–lined 12-unit muffin pan. Bake for 25 minutes.

❖ *Yield: twelve 2–4-ounce muffins or six 6–8-ounce muffins*

Chocolate Chip Muffins

This muffin is dedicated to all chocolate lovers. People love chocolate chips. Just notice the popularity of chocolate chip cookies and chocolate chip ice cream.

The lemon juice that I have included—a tip that comes from my mother—not only adds moisture to the muffin but also helps break up the eggs.

As for the variation that calls for mint to be added, it was an idea for Saint Patrick's Day. There was a desire for something green, so mint chocolate chip became the flavor theme. The peppermint extract plays off the chocolate in the same way as it does in peppermint chocolate chip ice cream. In the end, just about anything goes with chocolate.

2 cups flour
1 cup sugar
1 tablespoon baking powder
1 teaspoon salt
2 eggs
3/4 cup milk
1/4 cup oil

4 tablespoons butter or margarine, melted
1 teaspoon lemon juice
1/2 teaspoon corn syrup
1 teaspoon vanilla extract
1 cup (6 ounces) chocolate chips

Preheat the oven to 350 degrees. Sift together all the dry ingredients. Make a well in the center. Add the eggs, milk, oil, melted butter, lemon juice, and corn syrup and mix by hand. Fold in the vanilla and chocolate chips. Spoon into a wax paper–lined 12-unit muffin pan and bake for 25–30 minutes.

❖ *Yield: twelve 2–4-ounce muffins or six 6–8-ounce muffins*

Variation: For a mint chocolate chip taste and look, add 1 teaspoon peppermint extract and 3–4 drops green food coloring.

Chocolate chip muffins in the making

Black Bottom Muffins

It's funny how an everyday conversation with friends can spark a distinctive flavor combination. One day I was talking about that old dessert favorite known, at least around Baltimore, Maryland, and southern Pennsylvania, as "black bottom." It is a regular cake with chocolate chips planted in its bottom layer and cream cheese piped throughout the chocolate batter. That cake laid the foundation for the black bottom muffin. The earlier incarnations had the cream cheese on top as more of an icing, but once the cream cheese went on the inside, it really started taking shape.

2 cups flour

1 cup brown sugar

1 tablespoon baking powder

1 teaspoon salt

¼ cup unsweetened cocoa

¼ cup melted butter or margarine

¼ cup oil

¾ cup milk

2 eggs

1 teaspoon lemon juice

1 teaspoon vanilla extract

8 ounces cream cheese

1 cup (6 ounces) chocolate chips

Preheat the oven to 350 degrees. Sift together all the dry ingredients. Make a well in the center. Blend in the butter, oil, milk, eggs, lemon juice, and vanilla. Whip the cream cheese and put in a small pastry bag with a number 4 tip. Place 6 to 10 chocolate chips in each paper liner of a 12-unit muffin pan. Spoon the batter on top of the chips. Squeeze enough cream cheese into the batter so that it shows on top. Bake for 30–35 minutes.

❖ Yield: twelve 2–4-ounce muffins or six 6–8-ounce muffins

Chocolate-Strawberry Muffins

L et's say I have a bunch of strawberries just bursting with flavor. I start
to think of classic flavor combinations that everyone associates with
strawberries. Then it hits me: Who hasn't attended some kind of sophisticated
soiree and had one of those sinful chocolate-covered strawberries? And why
can't that wonderful taste combination be in a muffin?

2 cups flour
1 cup brown sugar
1 tablespoon baking powder
1 teaspoon salt
⅓ cup unsweetened cocoa
¼ pound (1 stick) butter or
*   margarine, melted*

¼ cup oil
¾ cup milk
2 eggs
1 teaspoon vanilla extract
1 teaspoon dark corn syrup
1 pint fresh strawberries

Sift together the dry ingredients. Make a well in the center. Add the
melted butter, oil, milk, eggs, vanilla, and corn syrup and blend well.
Spoon the batter into a wax paper–lined 12-unit muffin pan. Wash the
strawberries and place 1 or 2 in the center of each muffin. Bake for
35–40 minutes.

❖ *Yield: twelve 2–4-ounce muffins or six 6–8-ounce muffins*

Chocolate–White Chocolate Chunk Muffins

This recipe came from some leftover white chocolate I had used to garnish a wedding cake. The white chocolate had been in my refrigerator for a while, and I decided to get some use out of it by mixing it with chocolate batter.

White chocolate tends to be rather expensive. It really is a by-product of the process of making regular chocolate. After adding the cream to the regular chocolate and cooking it down, the white chocolate rises to the top of the chocolate. It is initially a foamy residue that one skims off. White chocolate is already naturally sweet, unlike raw cocoa, a bitter powder that needs to have cream and sugar added to it to become the sweet chocolate we all know.

White chocolate is a challenge to work with because it can separate easily. But there is no denying its new popularity. It used to be found only at fine chocolatiers or candy stores, but now you can find it on grocery shelves right next to the boxes of dark Baker's chocolate.

2 cups flour
1 cup sugar
1 tablespoon baking powder
1 teaspoon salt
1/4 cup unsweetened cocoa
3/4 cup milk
2 eggs

1/4 cup oil
4 tablespoons butter or margarine
1 teaspoon lemon juice
1/2 teaspoon corn syrup
1 teaspoon vanilla extract
3-4 squares white chocolate

Preheat the oven to 350 degrees. Sift together all the dry ingredients including the cocoa. Make a well in the center. Add the milk, eggs, oil, butter, lemon juice, corn syrup, and vanilla, and mix by hand. Using a well-sharpened knife, cut the white chocolate into chunks. Fold the chunks into the batter. Spoon the batter into a wax paper–lined 12-unit muffin pan and top off with additional chunks. Bake for 25–30 minutes.

❖ *Yield: twelve 2–4-ounce muffins or six 6–8-ounce muffins*

Glazed Orange Muffins

In this muffin, the buttermilk's acid interacts with the leavening ingredients of the muffin to give a better rise to the final muffin—though it doesn't affect the taste one bit. What's great is that when friends have milk that has turned sour, I'll say, "Sure, I'll use it. I can always use it." Sour milk works especially well with baking soda and with chocolate cake recipes.

The orange marmalade gives you the flavor of orange peel, and it certainly beats grating oranges. The jelly of the marmalade also acts as a moisturizer to the cake. When someone bites into a sliver of orange, they taste it, and it gives more credibility to the overall product. As a consumer I certainly know that I like to taste what I think I'm getting. If the label talks about oranges or parts of an orange, I expect to find that in the muffin. I think the rest of the public thinks just like me.

As for the glaze, it is important to poke holes in the muffin with a toothpick or fork while it is still hot. Pour the syrup over the muffins while they are in the pan so there is something to catch it. The syrup should go mostly inside the bread. It should be poured slowly, a teaspoon at a time, to ensure that the muffin absorbs the liquid. It's okay if it drizzles down the side between the muffin and the pan. But the pan's bottom shouldn't catch most of the syrup. That would be a waste of an excellent rum-flavored syrup.

½ cup orange juice

1 teaspoon rum flavoring

2 cups sugar

¼ pound (1 stick) butter or margarine

½ teaspoon baking soda

⅔ cup buttermilk

¼ teaspoon salt

2 cups flour

⅛ teaspoon mace

2 eggs

2 tablespoons orange marmalade

1 teaspoon vanilla extract

⅓ cup toasted, flaked coconut (see Piña Colada muffin recipe on page 64 for instructions on toasting)

Preheat the oven to 350 degrees. Mix the orange juice with the rum flavoring and 1 cup sugar in a saucepan. Heat over a low flame and stir to blend until the sugar is dissolved. Cream the remaining 1 cup sugar and butter. Dissolve the baking soda in the buttermilk. Sift together the salt, flour, and mace. Add the eggs, one at a time, to the creamed mixture. Alternately add the flour mix and buttermilk. Add the marmalade and vanilla. Fold in the toasted coconut. Spoon the batter into a wax paper–lined 12-unit muffin pan. Bake for 25–30 minutes. Remove from the oven and pour the orange juice mixture over each muffin, using approximately 2–4 tablespoons per muffin. Let stand 30 minutes before serving.

❖ *Yield: twelve 2–4-ounce muffins or six 6–8-ounce muffins*

Gingerbread

This was our first Christmas in my father's newly converted recreation room. Left to right: Brenda, me, and Olga.

The smell of ginger has its own romantic effect on people. When you think about gingerbread, you immediately think of Christmas, snow, Santa Claus, a crackling fire in front of you. All of these really cozy things come to mind. I distinctly remember my mom making gingerbread when I was a kid.

1 cup sugar

1 teaspoon salt

2 eggs

1 teaspoon baking soda

½ teaspoon cloves

½ cup margarine

½ cup molasses

2 cups flour

1 teaspoon cinnamon

⅛ teaspoon mace

1 teaspoon ginger

Confectioners' sugar (for dusting)

Preheat the oven to 350 degrees. Stir together all the ingredients. Pour in 1 cup boiling water. Mix and bake in a 4 by 8-inch loaf pan for 30 minutes. Dust with confectioners' sugar if desired.

❖ *Yield: 8–12 servings*

Molasses Loaf

In the past, granulated sugar was so valuable that people had to import it, and only the well-to-do could afford it. The regular populace had to make do with getting as much sugar as they could and converting it to molasses to make it last.

Everyone had molasses in their homes, for medicinal purposes if for nothing else. It's a nostalgic, cozy flavor.

²/₃ cup brown sugar
½ cup molasses
1 egg
1 teaspoon baking soda

²/₃ cup cold water
2 tablespoons butter, softened
1²/₃ cups flour

Preheat the oven to 350 degrees. Combine all the ingredients in the order given. Mix by hand. Do not beat. Spoon into a 4 by 8-inch loaf pan. Bake for 45 minutes. Serve warm with whipped cream.

❖ *Yield: 8–12 servings*

Supper Loaf

The intriguing name really has to do with how quickly you can throw this creation together so it's ready in time for supper. It is an easy cake to do and is served with whipped cream, no icing. This means you have something for dessert after preparing all the other elements of a real old-fashioned supper. It is very much in the spirit of those cake mixes, where you put everything in one pan and throw it in the oven. All those commercial products were drawn from recipes a little like this one.

2 cups brown sugar
¼ pound (1 stick) butter or
  margarine
2 cups flour
1 teaspoon baking soda
⅛ teaspoon mace
1 teaspoon salt

1 egg
1 cup buttermilk
1 teaspoon vanilla extract
¼ cup white sugar
1 teaspoon cinnamon
½ cup coarsely ground pecans

Preheat the oven to 350 degrees. Cream together the brown sugar and butter until light and fluffy. Sift together the flour, baking soda, mace, and salt. Add the egg to the creamed mixture. Alternately add the flour mix and buttermilk to the creamed mixture. Add the vanilla. Place in a greased or wax paper–lined 10 by 13-inch pan. Sprinkle the batter generously with the white sugar, cinnamon, and pecans. Bake for 30 minutes. Serve warm with whipped cream.

❖ *Yield: 8–12 servings*

Cupcakes and Cakes

E-Z Cupcakes

Why are they called "E-Z"? There just isn't a lot of creaming or sifting. It's a one-bowl job. You throw it all together and call it a day. Vanilla is its only flavoring, though variations might include almond, lemon, or orange flavoring. You don't have to lean toward vanilla just because I do. It happens to be my personal preference—vanilla is just so standard and reliable for most baked items, unless they contain a lot of other spices like nutmeg or cardamom.

1 egg
¼ pound (1 stick) butter or
*   margarine*
½ cup buttermilk
1 teaspoon baking soda

½ cup hot water
1¼ cups flour
1 teaspoon vanilla extract
1 cup sugar

Preheat the oven to 350 degrees. Place all the ingredients in a mixing bowl in the order given. Beat well at medium speed with an electric mixer. Fill 18 wax paper–lined muffin cups with the batter. Bake for 20 minutes.

❖ *Yield: 18 muffins*

Black Bottom Cupcakes

Basically, this is a variation of my black bottom muffins, only you don't have to worry about piping in the cream cheese. Just a dollop on top will do the trick.

1 cup plus 2 teaspoons sugar
1½ cups flour
1 teaspoon baking soda
¼ cup unsweetened cocoa
½ teaspoon salt

1 cup cold water
½ cup oil
1 tablespoon lemon juice
1 tablespoon vanilla extract
½ cup chopped nuts

Preheat the oven to 350 degrees. Sift together 1 cup sugar, flour, baking soda, cocoa, and salt. Blend in the cold water, oil, lemon juice, and vanilla. Spoon the batter into a wax paper–lined 12-unit muffin pan, approximately 4 tablespoons of batter per cup. Spoon approximately 1 tablespoon cream cheese mixture (recipe follows) on top of the batter. Combine the nuts and 2 teaspoons sugar, and sprinkle on the top. Bake for 35 minutes.

❖ Yield: 24 cupcakes

Cream Cheese Mixture

8 ounces cream cheese
1 egg
1/3 cup sugar
1/2 teaspoon salt

1 tablespoon vanilla extract
2 cups (12 ounces) chocolate
chips

Beat the cream cheese. Blend in the egg, sugar, salt, and vanilla. Stir in the chocolate chips.

Butterfly Cupcakes

For the butterfly design, slice off the top of the cupcake. Then, split the top in half and turn the two halves 180 degrees. The two round sides should be touching and the flat sides facing outward, making two butterfly wings.

½ cup flour

1 teaspoon baking powder

2 tablespoons instant coffee powder
   (decaffinated is optional)

⅛ teaspoon salt

12 tablespoons (1½ sticks) butter or
   margarine

½ cup granulated sugar

2 eggs

4½ ounces confectioners' sugar

1 teaspoon boiling water

Preheat the oven to 350 degrees. Sift the flour, baking powder, 1 tablespoon coffee, and salt. Cream 4 tablespoons (½ stick) butter with the granulated sugar until light and fluffy. Add the eggs one at a time. Gently fold in the flour mixture. Spoon the batter into a wax paper–lined 12-unit muffin pan and bake for 20–25 minutes. Let cool. Cream the remaining 8 tablespoons (1 stick) butter and 4 ounces (approximately ½ cup) confectioners' sugar until light and fluffy. Blend the remaining tablespoon coffee with the boiling water. Beat into the butter mixture. Cut a thin slice from the top of the cupcake and cut the slice in half. Dust heavily with the remaining confectioners' sugar. Coat the cupcakes with the icing. Arrange the cut slices to resemble a butterfly.

❖ *Yield: 1 dozen cupcakes*

Crumb Spice Cake

This is another quick-and-easy coffee cake, partially because you are not working with yeast. The buttermilk imparts acid and kicks in with its own special leavening, giving more height to the finished cake.

The "crumb" is a basic streusel. The good thing about a streusel topping is that since you probably have butter, brown sugar, and flour around already, it doesn't cause a lot of stress.

For the topping
2 cups flour
2 cups brown sugar
¼ pound (1 stick) butter or
*   margarine*

For the cake
1 egg, beaten
1 cup buttermilk
1 teaspoon baking soda
1 teaspoon cinnamon

Preheat the oven to 350 degrees. Mix the flour, brown sugar, and butter as for a pie crust. Reserve ⅔ cup for the topping. Using an electric mixer, blend the remaining ⅓ cup with the egg, buttermilk, baking soda, and cinnamon. Pour the batter into a 9 by 13-inch cake pan. Sprinkle the reserved mixture over the top. Bake for 25–30 minutes.

❖ *Yield: 8–12 servings*

German Coffee Cake

This dates back to my experimental first stages as a baker. I was attending many different coffee klatches thrown together by my girlfriends and me, and I was trying lots of different coffee cakes. We always experimented; sometimes it was with cocktails—how to mix the best piña colada—but we always threw ourselves into the baking, too.

The German part of this recipe is contained in the streusel. "Streusel" is the German term for crumb filling. In this case, the streusel is more of a topping involving chopped nuts. The eight ounces of sour cream really make this one heavy-duty cake. It is moist and doughy like any quick bread should be.

For the cake
¼ pound (1 stick) butter or
    margarine
1 cup sugar
2 eggs
1 teaspoon vanilla extract
1 teaspoon lemon juice
½ teaspoon almond extract
2 cups flour

1 teaspoon baking powder
1 teaspoon baking soda
¼ teaspoon salt
8 ounces sour cream

For the topping
¼ cup sugar
½ cup chopped nuts
2 teaspoons cinnamon
¼ teaspoon mace

Preheat the oven to 350 degrees. Cream the butter and sugar. Add the eggs. Add the vanilla, lemon juice, and almond extract. Sift together the flour, baking powder, baking soda, and salt. Alternately add the flour mixture and sour cream to the creamed mix. To make the topping, mix together the sugar, nuts, cinnamon, and mace. Spoon half of the batter into a wax paper–lined or well-greased tube pan. Sprinkle with half of the topping, spoon on the remaining batter, and cover with the remaining topping. Bake for 40 minutes.

❖ *Yield: 12–15 servings*

Maple Walnut Coffee Cake

I love this one because it immediately makes me think of pancakes and maple syrup. It gives you the syrup flavor without all the stickiness—the maple bakes right in.

When you are working with the yeast here, the water should be warm. It should dissolve at room temperature. The lukewarm water should be around 104 degrees. Yeast can't be allowed to get either too cold or too hot.

For the cake
1 package dry yeast
¾ cup warm water
¼ cup sugar
1 teaspoon salt
2¼ cups flour
1 egg
4 tablespoons butter or margarine, softened

For the topping
3 tablespoons butter or margarine, melted
¼ cup maple syrup
2 tablespoons brown sugar
3 tablespoons chopped walnuts or pecans

Preheat the oven to 350 degrees. Dissolve the yeast in the water in a mixing bowl. Add the sugar, salt, and half of the flour. Beat with an electric mixer at medium speed for about 2 minutes. Add the egg and butter. Beat in the remaining flour until smooth. To make the topping, mix together the butter, maple syrup, brown sugar, and nuts. Place the topping mix in a wax paper–lined 10-inch round cake pan. Drop small spoonfuls of batter over the topping, covering it. Cover the pan and let the batter rise in a warm place for approximately 1 hour, or until double in size. Bake for 30 minutes, or until brown. Remove from the oven and take out of the pan immediately.

❖ *Yield: 8–12 servings*

Working with yeast is always delicate.

Cream Cheese Holiday Cake

This is basically a cheese cake studded with your typical holiday candied fruits. For me, this cake immediately brings up feelings of Christmas.

Note that a springform pan, with its removable sides, works better than a tube pan because it allows easier removal of the cake.

8 ounces cream cheese	4 eggs
½ pound (2 sticks) butter or margarine	2¼ cups flour
	1½ teaspoons baking powder
1½ cups sugar	1 cup candied fruit
1½ teaspoons vanilla extract	½ cup chopped walnuts

Preheat the oven to 350 degrees. Blend the cream cheese, butter, sugar, vanilla, and eggs well. Sift 2 cups of the flour and the baking powder. Gradually add to the creamed mixture. Combine the remaining flour with the fruit and nuts. Fold into the batter. Bake in a springform pan for 45 minutes to 1 hour, or until a thin crust forms on the surface. Let cool 5 minutes.

❖ *Yield: 15 servings*

Mincemeat Applesauce Cake

I like mincemeat, and that, in a nutshell, explains the origins of this recipe. Mincemeat is really just candied meat, generally beef. It is very pungent, packing a strong taste.

Mincemeat is very easy to work with, and it bakes well. It has a great woodsy taste and works here the way meat dishes work with apple sauces.

*¼ pound (1 stick) butter
  or margarine
1 cup sugar
2 eggs
3 cups flour
1 teaspoon cinnamon*

*¼ teaspoon mace
2 teaspoons baking soda
¼ cup cold water
1 cup applesauce
1 cup nuts
1 cup mincemeat*

Preheat the oven to 350 degrees. Cream the butter and sugar. Add the eggs. Sift the flour, cinnamon, mace, and baking soda. Add the flour mix and water to the creamed mix. Add the applesauce. Mix in the nuts and mincemeat by hand. Pour into a greased or wax paper–lined 10-inch tube pan. Bake for 1 hour.

❖ *Yield: 15–20 servings*

My Favorite Cupcake Recipe

As a mother, is it any wonder that I would make cupcakes for my son when he was in kindergarten, first, second, and third grades? It was something for moms to do for class parties. I loved to add rainbow food coloring to them. It was my "Mommy contribution."

The variations coming out of this recipe, using chocolate chips and the food coloring, make baking really fun. It takes the boredom out of the work, and it allows you as a baker to make it colorful for your child.

I remember putting colors in my cupcakes long before Betty Crocker came along. I mean, I'm a mommy, and Betty Crocker and others got the ideas from somewhere—probably somebody's kitchen. You create the swirls by pulling a knife through the batter. It's fun to see all that color disperse throughout the batter once you've dipped the knife in. I don't tell anyone what colors to use. Personally, I prefer the basics, the primary colors of red, yellow, and blue. The only cautionary thing is that if you're not careful with your choices, you could end up with mud. But you will see what combinations work the best to create the nicest color designs.

4 eggs
2 cups sugar
¼ pound (1 stick) butter
1 cup milk

2 cups sifted flour
1 tablespoon baking powder
¼ teaspoon salt
1 tablespoon vanilla extract

Preheat the oven to 350 degrees. Beat the eggs. Gradually add the sugar. Melt the butter. Add the milk to the heated butter. Sift together the flour, baking powder, and salt. Alternately add the milk and flour mixture to the beaten eggs. Add the vanilla. Spoon 2–3 tablespoons of batter into a wax paper–lined 12-unit muffin pan. Bake for 20–25 minutes. Remove, cool, and ice.

❖ *Yield: two dozen 2–3-ounce cupcakes*

Variations: Add 1 cup of chocolate chips to the batter.

For a rainbow effect, add 2 ounces of multicolored nonpareils or droplets of red, blue, or yellow food coloring. Do not stir. Use a knife and cut through the batter. After gently spooning into the muffin pan, the colors will disperse separately.

My Favorite Frosting

This is the recipe that chefs have been trying to pry away from me for years. I mean, at one point people were offering to buy this frosting from me. I created this recipe completely, back in Rochester, New York, for a child's birthday cake. I wanted to try to re-create the richness of a whipped cream icing without having to deal with volatile whipped cream.

Here's the secret: You have to whip your ingredients at the highest speed your mixer can handle. The creaming must be done vigorously, gradually adding the confectioners' sugar. And notice that the confectioners' sugar must be weighed because it is its *weight* and not its measurement that counts here.

½ pound (2 sticks) butter or margarine
¼ cup heavy sour cream

2 teaspoons vanilla extract
8 ounces confectioners' sugar

A kitchen scale comes in handy for weighing out powdered sugar.

With an electric mixer, cream the butter until light and fluffy. Add the sour cream and continue to cream until light and fluffy. Add the vanilla. Gradually add the sugar. Whip until stiff peaks form.

❖ *Yield: enough for 1 layer cake or 2 dozen cupcakes*

Sour Cream Coffee Cake

This is a tube pan creation that can also work in a Bundt pan. These kinds of pans were designed specifically for baked goods that require heating in the center to complete the baking process.

For the cake
1/4 pound (1 stick) butter or
    margarine
1 cup sugar
2 eggs
1 teaspoon baking powder
1/4 teaspoon salt
2 cups flour

1 teaspoon baking soda
8 ounces sour cream
1 teaspoon vanilla extract
For the topping
1/4 cup sugar
1 teaspoon cinnamon
1/2 cup nuts, chopped

Preheat the oven to 350 degrees. Cream the butter and sugar. Add the eggs. Mix together the dry ingredients. Alternately add them with the sour cream and vanilla to the creamed mixture. To make the topping, mix together the sugar, cinnamon, and nuts. Pour half of the batter into a greased and floured 10-inch round tube pan. Sprinkle half of the topping on the batter. Add the remaining batter and sprinkle with the remaining topping. Bake 35 to 40 minutes.

❖ *Yield: 15–20 servings*

Spice Coffee Cake

This is a real northern New York State kind of quick bread, inspired by the wintry weather. Remember that people in a rough winter climate are going to eat a lot of fat, such as butter, eggs, and sour cream, in order to deal with the cold.

The sourness doesn't ever come through from the sour cream. What does happen is that its particular acid acts as another leavening ingredient. Really, sour cream works the same way cultured buttermilk does.

This dish is also presented in a tube pan, which can come in the form of a bundt pan. The standard tube pan often has a drop-out bottom, which makes it easier to unmold.

For the cake
½ teaspoon salt
2 cups flour
1 teaspoon baking powder
1 teaspoon baking soda
½ pound (2 sticks) butter or
    margarine
1 cup sugar

2 eggs
1 teaspoon vanilla extract
8 ounces sour cream
For the topping
½ cup chopped walnuts
½ cup brown sugar
1 teaspoon cinnamon
1 teaspoon nutmeg

Preheat the oven to 350 degrees. Sift together the salt, flour, baking powder, and soda. Cream together the butter and sugar. Add the eggs and vanilla. Alternately add the flour mixture and sour cream to the creamed mix. For the topping, combine the topping ingredients in the order given.

Pour half of the batter into a wax paper–lined 10-inch round tube pan. Sprinkle half of the topping on the batter. Add the remaining batter and sprinkle with the remaining topping. Bake for 45 minutes.

❖ *Yield: 15–20 servings*

Streusel-Filled Coffee Cake

This coffee cake looks a lot like what you might buy at a commercial grocer or bakery, but the taste says "homemade."

For the cake
1½ cups flour
1 tablespoon baking powder
¼ teaspoon salt
¾ cup white sugar
4 tablespoons butter or margarine
1 egg
½ cup milk
1 teaspoon vanilla extract

For the filling and topping
½ cup brown sugar
2 tablespoons flour
2 teaspoons cinnamon
2 tablespoons melted butter or margarine
½ cup chopped nuts

Preheat the oven to 350 degrees. Sift the dry ingredients. Slice the butter into pieces and use a knife to stir them into the dry ingredients until a fine cornmeal-like mixture is attained. Mix together the egg, milk, and vanilla, and add to the flour mixture. To make the topping, mix together the brown sugar, flour, and cinnamon. Blend in the butter and nuts. Spread half of the batter in a wax paper–lined 8-inch square pan. Sprinkle with half of the topping. Add the remaining batter and cover with the remaining topping. Bake for 25–35 minutes.

❖ *Yield: 8–12 servings*

Cookies and Pastries

Bethlehem Rolls

This is another Christmas item that also originates from Pennsylvania. It's from the town of Hazleton, which really does Christmas right. There is lots of baking going on there all the time, and they still do the Christmas tree with the train tracks running around it. People still make their own chocolates especially for the season.

There is some yeast involved in this recipe, yet it is still a quick one. You have to be careful anytime you use yeast, but other than crumbling up the yeast cake, there is no hot water to be poured, so the yeast really works itself.

½ pound (2 sticks) butter
½ pound margarine
4 eggs, well beaten
1 small yeast cake, crumbled
8 ounces sour cream

4 cups flour
1 cup confectioners' sugar (for dusting)
1 cup finely chopped walnuts or pecans

Melt the butter and margarine. Combine with the eggs, yeast cake, sour cream, and flour, and mix until the dough is sticky. Refrigerate for 6–8 hours. Preheat the oven to 350 degrees. Roll little pieces separately in the confectioners' sugar and then in the nuts. Place on a cookie sheet. Bake for 10–12 minutes.

❖ *Yield: 4–6 dozen*

Butter Chews

There is certainly a lot of butter in this recipe, a little short of two sticks' worth. In a word, butter is fattening. It has quite a distinct taste from margarine, so it is difficult to find a spread, or any other substitute, that quite matches butter—certainly for this recipe.

12 tablespoons (1½ sticks)
 soft butter
3 tablespoons sugar
1½ cups flour
3 eggs, separated

2¼ cups light brown sugar, packed
1 cup chopped walnuts
¾ cup flaked coconut
½ cup confectioners' sugar

Preheat the oven to 350 degrees. Cream the butter and sugar. Blend in the flour. Spread evenly on a 13 by 9 by 2-inch pan. Bake for 15 minutes. Beat the egg whites until stiff but not dry. Set aside. Beat the egg yolks until thick and lemon-colored, about 10 minutes. Beat in the brown sugar. Fold in the chopped nuts and coconut. Fold in the reserved egg whites. Spread the mixture over the baked layer. Bake for 25–30 minutes. Cool. Dust with confectioners' sugar and cut into squares.

❖ *Yield: 8–12 servings*

Butterscotch Chews

Butterscotch is one of those reminders of my youth. The "chewiness" of this creation is in the amount of butter used. This is one dense, sweet confection.

¼ pound (1 stick) butter
2 cups brown sugar
2 eggs, beaten
1 cup flour
1 teaspoon baking powder

¼ teaspoon salt
½ cup chopped walnuts
1 teaspoon vanilla extract
Confectioners' sugar (for dusting)

Preheat the oven to 350 degrees. Melt the butter in a large saucepan. Add the sugar and beaten eggs. Let cool. Add the flour, baking powder, salt, nuts, and vanilla. Spread in a well-greased 9 by 9 by 2-inch pan. Bake for 25 minutes. Let cool for 10 minutes after removing from the oven. Dust with confectioners' sugar and cut into squares.

❖ *Yield: 8–12 servings*

Melting butter for butterscotch chews

Caramel-Nut Squares

I remember every step of my childhood ritual—from going into the department store and seeing how the caramels were measured out and separated into quarter-pound piles. Caramel and butterscotch are two of the premier tastes from my youth.

½ pound (2 sticks) melted butter or margarine
2 cups brown sugar
2 eggs

1¼ cups flour
1 teaspoon vanilla extract
1 cup chopped pecans
Confectioners' sugar (for dusting)

Preheat the oven to 350 degrees. Pour the butter over the sugar. Beat until light and fluffy. Add the eggs, flour, and vanilla. Fold in the nuts. Pour into 9-inch square pan. Bake for 35–40 minutes. Sprinkle with confectioners' sugar. Cut into squares when cool.

❖ *Yield: 8–12 servings*

Chocolate Chip Cookies

The texture of this chocolate chip cookie makes it different. It is not a hard cookie. It is soft and has a cakelike texture when you bite into it.

2 cups flour
1½ cups brown sugar
1 teaspoon baking powder
½ teaspoon salt
½ pound (2 sticks) butter or
   margarine

2 eggs
2 teaspoons vanilla extract
2 cups (12 ounces) chocolate chips

Preheat the oven to 350 degrees. Sift together the flour, sugar, baking powder, and salt. Cut the butter into the flour mixture until pea-size balls form. Mix in the eggs and vanilla. Fold in the chocolate chips. Drop by teaspoonfuls onto a wax paper–lined or greased baking sheet. Bake for 8–10 minutes.

❖ Yield: 3½ dozen

Choco-Marshmallow Cookies

M arshmallow is fun to work with because it breaks down easily. You can actually make your own marshmallows if you want, since they are nothing more than egg whites and sugar, but this gets into the area of candy, which is very complex. It is much easier to go to the store and buy a bag of marshmallows.

I think marshmallows and cocoa is a great combination. I just automatically think of "smores."

For the cookies

1¾ cups flour

½ teaspoon salt

½ teaspoon baking soda

½ cup unsweetened cocoa

¼ pound (1 stick) butter or
  margarine

1 cup sugar

1 egg

1 teaspoon vanilla extract

¼ cup evaporated milk

1 bag (12 ounces) large
  marshmallows

For the icing

2 cups confectioners' sugar, sifted

5 tablespoons unsweetened cocoa

⅛ teaspoon salt

3 tablespoons butter or margarine,
  softened

4-5 tablespoons light cream or
  evaporated milk

Preheat the oven to 350 degrees. Sift together the flour, salt, baking soda, and cocoa. Cream the butter and sugar. Blend in the egg, vanilla, and milk. Mix in the dry ingredients. Drop by teaspoonful onto a wax paper–lined or greased cookie sheet. Bake for 8–10 minutes. Cut the marshmallows in half and press, cut side down, on the hot cookies. Bake 2 minutes longer.

For the icing: Combine the sugar, cocoa, and salt. Mix in the softened butter and light cream. Dip the warm cookies in the icing.

❖ *Yield: 2–3 dozen*

Coconut Cookies

The same sister-in-law who gave me the recipe for a tomato soup muffin provided me with this one as well. She loves to have me try recipes of hers, because she knows I do this for a living. Any home baker feels proud when a pro does something they've done. Like me, she's a real home baker.

4 tablespoons butter

1 cup sugar

1 egg, beaten

1 pound dates, cut into 1-inch pieces

2 cups toasted rice cereal (e.g., Rice Krispies)

½ cup nuts, chopped

14 ounces coconut, flaked

Combine the butter, sugar, egg, and dates in a saucepan. Bring to a boil, then lower the heat to medium and cook for 2 minutes. Add the cereal and nuts, and blend them in. Oil or butter your hands and form the mixture into balls. Roll the balls in the coconut.

❖ *Yield: 2–3 dozen*

Congo Squares

Butterscotch was a candy my mother always bought when we were kids. I remember going with her to Woodward and Lothrop to do most of our shopping. It was at Woody's that I was mesmerized by the bakers in the bake shop section. All that baking was going on in front of my face, and I could see it and smell it.

Those hard butterscotch candies were always a treat, wrapped in cellophane that we couldn't open until we had finished our dinner. Boy, the way our mother held us hostage over those pieces of candy! It worked—we did her bidding throughout the rest of the day. It was a big deal to us, and it explains my fondness for butterscotch in my baking.

½ pound (2 sticks) butter or margarine
1 pound brown sugar
3 eggs
1 cup pecans, chopped

6 ounces butterscotch morsels
2¾ cups flour
2½ teaspoons baking powder
½ teaspoon salt

Preheat the oven to 350 degrees. Cream the butter, brown sugar, and eggs. Fold in the remaining ingredients. Spread on a greased and floured 9 by 13-inch pan. Bake for 30 minutes. Cut into squares 10 minutes after removing from the oven. Remove from the pan when completely cooled and separate the squares.

❖ *Yield: 8–12 servings*

Cookie Bars

These are really caught somewhere between a cookie and a bar cookie. They are remarkably moist and chewy.

½ pound (2 sticks) butter or
    margarine
½ cup white sugar
1½ cups brown sugar
2 eggs, separated
1 tablespoon water
1 teaspoon vanilla extract

2 cups flour
¼ teaspoon salt
1 teaspoon baking powder
¼ teaspoon baking soda
1 cup (6 ounces) chocolate chips
4 ounces coconut, flaked
2 egg whites

Cream the butter with the white sugar and ½ cup brown sugar. Add the egg yolks, water, and vanilla. Sift the flour, salt, baking powder, and baking soda. Blend into the creamed mixture to form a stiff dough. Press by hand onto a cookie sheet. Sprinkle with chocolate chips. Beat the egg whites into stiff peaks, gradually adding the remaining cup brown sugar. Spread over the chocolate chips. Sprinkle with coconut. Bake for 20–25 minutes or until the coconut is browned. When completely cool, cut into bars or squares.

❖ Yield: 4–5 dozen cookies

Crisp Toffee Bars

When you think of toffee, what immediately comes to mind is probably something really, really chewy that ends up getting stuck to your teeth and the roof of your mouth.

Toffee is basically sugar that has been worked over in some fashion. The chocolate chips and walnuts are my variation on the English original.

½ pound (2 sticks) butter or margarine
1 cup brown sugar
1 teaspoon vanilla extract

1 teaspoon rum flavoring
2 cups flour
1 cup (6 ounces) chocolate chips
1 cup chopped walnuts

Preheat the oven to 350 degrees. Cream the butter, sugar, vanilla, and rum flavoring. Add the flour. Stir in the chocolate chips and nuts. Press into an ungreased 9 by 13-inch pan. Bake for 25 minutes. Cut into bars 10 minutes after removing from the oven. When completely cooled, remove from pan and separate bars.

❖ *Yield: 8–12 servings*

Favorite Christmas Cookie

This cookie is like biting into pie crust. It is really light, and you get that by baking it no longer than the time allotted. This is a cookie you really have to watch. It bakes very quickly and will appear not to be done because it might still look white on top. But it is ready. The cookie rises and then falls back down, but it still has that firmness. Personally, I like to use a cookie cutter for my favorite designs. For decorating these cookies, a pastry bag can be used to create some eye-catching designs. Try making snowmen and decorating them. Make colored sugar by taking a scoop and dropping food coloring in it. With droplets of coloring, it is easier to control how deep a coloring you get. If you put in too much, the sugar will be too wet. Two or three droplets will give you the kind of color you are looking for. Red and green are the perfect Christmas colors. You shouldn't throw the colored sugar away but instead keep it for the next project. These cookies make ideal Christmas cookie tray items.

I use this cookie to decorate my gingerbread houses because I don't like putting candy on the house. These cookies become the windows and doors and other accoutrements attached to the house. Because they are sturdy yet light, they are a great gingerbread-house addition.

*½ pound (2 sticks) butter or
    margarine*
⅔ cup sugar
2 eggs
1 teaspoon vanilla extract

3 cups flour
½ teaspoon salt
1 teaspoon baking powder
Colored sugar

Cream the butter and sugar. Add the eggs and beat well. Add the vanilla.
Sift together the flour, salt, and baking powder. Add the flour mixture
to the creamed mixture. Chill approximately 2 hours. Preheat the oven to
350 degrees. Add your favorite food coloring by droplet to white sugar and
mix to make colored sugar. Roll out the dough to ¼-inch thickness and
sprinkle with the colored sugar. Press the sugar into the dough with a rolling
pin. Cut out the dough in your favorite shapes. Bake for 5–7 minutes.

❖ *Yield: depends on size of cookie
cutter used*

"Anybody want to buy a muffin?"

Favorite Sugar Cookie

This is another recipe that I toyed with. It slowly developed into my favorite, partially because it became everyone else's favorite. When I first made this cookie, my daughters told me that it reminded them of the sugar cookie sold at that time that had a brown edge around it. Woodward and Lothrop's bakery department and Pepperidge Farm came out with sugar cookies that looked the same way.

I found out about these cookies by accident. I didn't have anybody else's recipe, of course, but I started experimenting with how thin I could make these cookies. The less flour, the thinner the cookies became. I ended up making them as thin as a chip. That rounded cup of flour can be leveled off to give you a thinner cookie, since this recipe is sensitive to using even a half a teaspoon less flour. In any case, you should always end up with a cookie that has a nice light brown edge to it.

And although these cookies are very thin, you still get a chewy, crisp texture that is moist. It really is a great cookie.

2 rounded or leveled cups flour
1½ cups sugar
1 teaspoon baking powder
½ teaspoon salt

½ pound (2 sticks) butter or
  margarine
2 eggs
2 teaspoons vanilla extract

Preheat the oven to 350 degrees. Sift together the flour, sugar, baking powder, and salt. Cut the butter into the flour mixture until small pea-size balls form. Make a well in the center and add the eggs and vanilla. With a spoon or by hand, mix together until a soft dough forms. Drop the dough by teaspoonful onto a cookie sheet—no more than 1 dozen per sheet. Bake for 8–10 minutes, or until golden brown around the edges.

❖ *Yield: 4 dozen*

Variation: Roll the dough balls in Baker's unsweetened cocoa or a combination of cocoa and confectioners' sugar.

German Cream Cheese Brownies

This recipe is a bit of a takeoff on German chocolate cake, using semisweet chocolate. It is the same taste sensation as most of your chocolate chips, which are semisweet as well.

When it comes to using the double boiler, remember that real chocolate should never be melted over direct heat. It will burn too fast. The best way is in the top of a double boiler, meaning over indirect heat. Another quick way to do it is in the microwave, but that is a judgment call. Make sure it isn't in the microwave more than a minute, and watch it all the time.

The cream cheese makes for a nice presentation: When you slice into the brownies, the entire thing looks like a large Oreo cookie with cream cheese as the filling.

5 tablespoons butter or margarine
4 ounces German chocolate
3 ounces cream cheese
½ cup white sugar
3 eggs
½ cup plus 1 tablespoon flour
1 teaspoon vanilla extract

½ cup brown sugar
½ teaspoon baking powder
¼ teaspoon salt
1 teaspoon rum flavoring
½ cup chopped walnuts
1 cup (6 ounces) chocolate chips

Preheat the oven to 350 degrees. Melt 3 tablespoons butter and the chocolate in the top of a double boiler. Stir and let cool. Cream the remaining 2 tablespoons butter with the cream cheese. Gradually beat in ¼ cup of the white sugar until light and fluffy. Blend in 1 egg, 1 tablespoon flour, and the vanilla. Beat the remaining 2 eggs until light and fluffy, about 10 minutes. Gradually add the brown sugar and remaining ¼ cup white sugar until the mixture thickens. Add the baking powder, salt, and remaining ½ cup flour. Fold in the chocolate mixture, rum flavoring, and nuts. Spread half of the batter onto a wax paper–lined or greased 9 by 9 by 2-inch pan. Top with the cream cheese mixture. Sprinkle with the chocolate chips. Spoon the remaining batter on top. Zigzag a knife through for a marble effect. Bake for 35 to 40 minutes.

❖ *Yield: 8–12 servings*

E-Z Cookie Bars

These deserve their name because they are truly easy to make. Another Mom's original, this made its first appearance during those coffee klatches with my friends in my old housewife days. Those were the days: living in that sixteen-story high rise, and if our husbands didn't take us out, we brought the outside world into our living rooms.

The graham cracker crumbs bring their own special flavor. They bring cinnamon to the table, which enhances anything. The crumbs naturally become an instant crust, baking nicely in the pan and forming a nice crispy base.

¼ pound (1 stick) butter or margarine
1½ cups graham cracker crumbs
1 can (14 ounces) sweetened condensed milk

1 cup (6 ounces) chocolate chips
1 4-ounce can coconut
1 cup chopped walnuts

Preheat the oven to 350 degrees. Melt the butter in a 13 by 9-inch pan in the oven. Sprinkle the crumbs over the butter. Pour the milk over the crumbs. Top with the remaining ingredients and press down firmly. Bake for 25–30 minutes. Let cool before cutting into 18 rectangular pieces.

❖ *Yield: 18 servings*

Fudge Squares

The dark corn syrup used here adds moisture to the squares and binds their ingredients together. The old-fashioned oats are like the rolled oats in that it takes them longer to absorb any moisture. In fact, rolled oats are even less refined than old-fashioned oats. In any case, because of that longer absorption time, the rolled oats will give more texture to your fudge.

2 ounces unsweetened chocolate
1/3 cup butter or margarine
1/4 cup dark corn syrup
2/3 cup sugar

1/2 teaspoon salt
1 1/2 teaspoons vanilla extract
2 cups old-fashioned oats
1/4 cup chopped walnuts

Preheat the oven to 350 degrees. Melt the chocolate and butter in the top of a double boiler. Add the remaining ingredients and blend thoroughly. Press the mixture firmly into an oiled or wax paper–lined 8 by 8 by 2-inch pan. Bake for 15–20 minutes. Let cool and cut into squares.

❖ *Yield: 8–12 servings*

Gingerbread Cookies

At Christmas you always think of gingerbread men. You do your shapes, and then you fill up the pastry bag to finish them off. It is easy to use the pastry bag for creating Christmas characters such as angels and Santa Clauses. Eventually, you graduate to a gingerbread house.

Interestingly, when I was making one of my first gingerbread houses, I would trim it, collecting sheets and strips of gingerbread and throwing them in a bowl and a nearby basket. My son and his friends would come into the kitchen and start eating the thin gingerbread pieces. They liked them so much that they suggested I sell the scraps—they were that good.

½ pound (2 sticks) butter or
   margarine, melted
½ cup dark corn syrup
1 cup sugar
1 egg
2 teaspoons baking soda

1 teaspoon cardamom
1 teaspoon ginger
1 teaspoon cloves
1 teaspoon cinnamon
3 tablespoons evaporated milk
3 cups flour

Combine the melted butter with the corn syrup. Add the remaining ingredients and mix well. Refrigerate for 5–6 hours. Preheat the oven to 350 degrees. Roll out the dough and sprinkle it liberally with colored sugar. Press the sugar in by using a rolling pin. Cut the dough into desired shapes and bake on a sheet for 8–10 minutes.

❖ *Yield: depends on the size of the shapes used*

Heavenly Layer Cookies

This is another bar item transformed into a cookie. This one in particular is distinguished by its layers. You might call it a "blondie."

The graham cracker crumbs make for the real bar, added to a cookie crust. When you throw in the chocolate and butterscotch chips, you get pure decadence. I just love that butterscotch—and all the remembrances of childhood that spill from it. And the shredded coconut is also a throwback to my mother's coconut cake, topped with that real old-fashioned seven-minute icing. It was, and remains, the real deal.

4 tablespoons butter or margarine,
    melted
1 cup graham cracker crumbs
1 cup (6 ounces) chocolate chips

1 cup (6 ounces) butterscotch chips
1 cup shredded coconut
1 cup chopped walnuts
1 can sweetened condensed milk

Preheat the oven to 350 degrees. Pour the butter into a 9 by 13-inch pan. Press the graham cracker crumbs onto the bottom of the pan. Add the chocolate and butterscotch chips, coconut, and nuts in layers. Drizzle the milk over the top. Bake for 30 minutes. Cut into squares.

❖ *Yield: 2 dozen*

Macaroon Drops

The condensed milk used here is the classic Borden's sweetened condensed milk that has the consistency of syrup and is absolutely saturated with sugar.

This is very much like a coconut macaroon recipe, with the almond extract giving it a macaroonlike flavor and essence. A real macaroon, however, requires almond paste and has an almond in the center of it.

Since this particular recipe involves so much coconut, you can put this in the oven and it will never get hard.

1 cup sweetened condensed milk
4 cups shredded coconut
⅛ teaspoon salt

2 teaspoons vanilla extract
¼ teaspoon almond extract

Preheat the oven to 350 degrees. Combine all the ingredients. Drop by teaspoonful onto a wax paper–lined cookie sheet. Bake for 8–10 minutes.

❖ *Yield: 3–4 dozen*

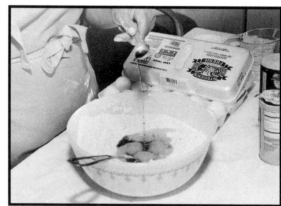

Vanilla—a key ingredient in almost all of my baking—caught in mid-drip.

Meringue Cookies

This recipe dates from my Rochester, New York, days. I remember going to a particular P.T.A. meeting where a lot of women attending were homemakers. One woman there, among the many who were working part-time jobs, recommended this recipe. It is designed as a light dessert and a complement to coffee.

Beat the egg whites as stiff as possible. Egg whites must be whipped until they are rigid and nearly dry. When you turn the bowl upside down, the egg whites should remain where they are. That is the test the pros use.

1 egg white
⅛ teaspoon salt
⅔ cup sugar

1 teaspoon vanilla extract
1 cup chopped walnuts
1 cup (6 ounces) chocolate chips

Preheat the oven to 350 degrees. Beat the egg white and salt until soft peaks form. Gradually add the sugar and vanilla. Fold in the nuts and chocolate chips. Drop by teaspoonful onto wax paper–lined cookie sheet. Turn off the oven, place the cookies in the oven, and let sit for 3 or more hours.

❖ *Yield: 3–4 dozen*

Mint Brownies

This is a Girl Scout cookies–inspired recipe. I started out as a Brownie scout and made it all the way to Girl Scout. I remember selling those mint chocolate cookies. They are a timeless classic.

Mint is such a southern thing. I mean, we had it growing wild in our yard—perfect for great iced mint tea and mint juleps. You always had to have a sprig of mint in there. It's just a very southern tradition, and I am the daughter of a southern belle.

Baker's chocolate is used here because, like cocoa, it has no sugar in it. You can control the sweetness with how much sugar you add. As for the peppermint flavoring, you can find that in the grocery store. A new wrinkle would be to add the mint chocolate chips that are now on the market.

It's best to spread the icing with a spatula. This is not a drizzle icing, where you would be better off with a fork.

For the brownies
1/4 pound (1 stick) butter or
   margarine
1 1/2 ounces Baker's chocolate
1 cup sugar
1/2 cup flour
1/8 teaspoon salt
2 eggs
1/2 teaspoon peppermint flavoring

For the icing
2 tablespoons butter or margarine
1 tablespoon light cream
1 cup confectioners' sugar
3/4 teaspoon peppermint flavoring
Green food coloring

Preheat the oven to 350 degrees. Melt the butter and Baker's chocolate together. Sift the sugar, flour, and salt. Beat in the eggs. Add the chocolate mixture and peppermint flavoring. Pour into a wax paper–lined or greased and floured 8-inch square pan. Bake for 25 minutes. To make the icing, blend all the ingredients with an electric mixer until smooth. Spread the icing onto the warm brownies. Cut into squares when cool.

❖ *Yield: 8–12 servings*

Peanut Butter Fluffs

The egg whites here must be very stiff. After all, whipped egg whites are what add air to the fluffs. Considering that the peanut butter adds weight and makes it heavy, the lightness from the egg whites functions like a balloon, lifting the other stuff up, giving it height.

1 cup creamy peanut butter
1 cup sugar
1 teaspoon vanilla extract

⅛ teaspoon salt
3 egg whites, beaten stiff

Preheat the oven to 300 degrees. Cream together the peanut butter, sugar, vanilla, and salt. Fold in the egg whites. Drop by teaspoonful onto a wax paper–lined or greased cookie sheet. Bake for 20 minutes.

❖ *Yield: 3 dozen*

Peanut Butter Cookies

This is a traditional peanut butter cookie recipe with that crisscross pattern in the center. We all remember that little checkerboard done with a fork. And you really don't mess with the original, because nothing beats it.

Chilling the dough allows it to set and take on a different color and texture. It allows the solid fat to resettle. You notice this effect when you take melted butter and chill it; it will set up yet again. As for the chilled dough, overall it acts as an adhesive, pulling all the grains together. It is its own cement.

Bakers are like people who build houses. We make cement blocks and the mortar to bind the building together. If our cement—the dough—gets sticky, just dust the dough with flour, and it will come back together.

1/4 pound (1 stick) butter or margarine, softened	*1 1/4 cups flour*
1/2 cup peanut butter	*1/2 teaspoon baking powder*
1/2 cup light brown sugar (packed)	*3/4 teaspoon baking soda*
1 egg	*1/4 teaspoon salt*
	1/8 teaspoon mace

Cream the butter, peanut butter, brown sugar, and egg. Sift together the dry ingredients and gradually add to the creamed mixture. Chill for 1 1/2 hours. Preheat the oven to 350 degrees. Roll the dough out and form into walnut-size pieces. Place 3 inches apart on a wax paper–lined cookie sheet. Flatten them. Crisscross with a fork dipped in flour. Bake for 8–10 minutes.

❖ *Yield: 3 dozen*

Rum Balls

The origin of this recipe comes from my days of dealing with a wonderful Italian restaurant in Rochester, New York. At one point the owner asked me if I could prepare for him a baba au rhum dessert. It's a briochelike roll positively soaked in rum. It then has to have some kind of filling, usually a cream concoction. I prefer to fill mine with a version of an Italian meringue. Even ricotta cheese blended with confectioners' sugar can be used. But the most important thing is that the bread be absolutely soaked in rum.

Now, I didn't really appreciate all this at the time. I was still being introduced to real Italian baking. What I brought to the restaurant owner was the following recipe, which turned out to be rum balls.

For those who shy away from using alcohol in their desserts, you can substitute a quarter cup of water mixed with a healthy tablespoon of rum flavoring for the rum. The sugar cookies that have been included in this collection are really key to this recipe working. They are very rich, and the rest of the recipe contains no butter.

1 dozen Favorite Sugar Cookies
  (page 192)
¼ cup honey
1 cup (6 ounces) chocolate chips
1 teaspoon vanilla extract

2 cups coarsely ground walnuts
⅓ cup rum
1-2 cups unsweetened cocoa
  (enough to roll rum balls
  around in)

Heat the honey and the chocolate chips in the top of a double boiler until the chocolate has melted. Remove from the heat. Add the vanilla. Break the sugar cookies into small pieces by hand. Combine with the walnuts and rum. Shape the mixture into 1- or 2-inch balls. Roll them in the cocoa. Store in a tightly covered container overnight. They can be served in as little as 3 or 4 hours.

❖ *Yield: 3½ dozen of 1-inch size; 1¾ dozen of 2-inch size*

Buns freshly drizzled with icing

Rum Spice Buns

My son's best friend approached me one day and asked if I could make some cinnamon buns. He said something like "Oh, please, Miss Linda. They are so good," so I couldn't deny his request.

The result has sparked quite a bit of nostalgia, I must say. What happens is that people in their seventies who try one of them immediately smile and say it reminds them of what their grandparents made. It just goes to show what an enduring classic these sweet rolls are.

For the dough
2 packages dry yeast
⅓ cup warm water
¼ pound (1 stick) butter or margarine
¾ cup milk
1¼ teaspoons salt
½ cup granulated sugar
3 eggs
6 cups flour

For the filling
1 cup light brown sugar
1 cup granulated sugar
2¼ teaspoons cinnamon
1¼ teaspoons nutmeg

¼ cup flour
¼ pound (1 stick) butter or margarine

For the icing
2 tablespoons brown sugar
⅓ cup evaporated milk
1 teaspoon vanilla extract
1 teaspoon rum flavoring
1 pound confectioners' sugar

Dissolve the yeast in the water. Let sit for 10 minutes. In a saucepan, melt the butter with the milk, salt, and sugar. Set aside to cool until lukewarm. Combine the yeast and milk mixtures in a mixing bowl either by hand or with an electric mixer with a dough hook attachment at low speed. Add the eggs. Gradually blend in 5 cups flour, until a very sticky dough forms. Make sure the flour is well blended and has a pastelike consistency. Add the remaining 1 cup flour, ½ cup at a time, until the dough is cohesive but no longer sticky. Knead the dough by hand for 10 minutes or by machine, using a dough hook, for 5 minutes. Remove the dough from the bowl, place it in another well-oiled bowl, and cover with plastic wrap or a towel. Keep the bowl in a warm (not hot) place until the dough has doubled in size, up to 1 hour.

To make the filling: Combine all the ingredients except the butter. Cut the butter into little pieces and toss the mixture by hand until small pea-size balls form.

Remove the dough and place it on a lightly floured surface. Roll it out until it is approximately 30 by 10 inches. Spread the filling on the rolled-out dough, then roll up the dough along the 30-inch side toward you until it is completely

Buttering buns before icing

rolled up. Cut the dough widthwise into 12 even disks. Place the disks 2 inches apart on a wax paper–lined or well-greased and floured cookie sheet. Cover with a towel and set in a warm place and let rise for 1 hour. Preheat the oven to 350 degrees. Bake the disks for 20 minutes.

To make the icing: Combine the brown sugar and evaporated milk in a saucepan and let come to a boil. Remove from the heat. Add the vanilla and rum flavoring. Stir in the confectioners' sugar until the desired thickness is reached. Drizzle over the hot rolls.

Optional Step: For extra-rich buns, brush on ½ stick (4 tablespoons) melted butter before icing.

Pastries

The cream cheese used here and in so many of my recipes ends up being almost like a butter substitute. What it lacks is the overwhelming fat content of butter—and the cream cheese works just as well. Anybody will tell you that if there is anything about Linda's cakes, they are all rich.

You can use a sifter to dust these with confectioners' sugar. You need to achieve a heavy layer, coating them like a blanket of snow.

½ pound (2 sticks) butter
8 ounces cream cheese

2 cups flour
Confectioners' sugar (for dusting)

Preheat the oven to 350 degrees. Cream the butter and cream cheese with the flour. Roll out onto a floured surface to a ¼-inch thickness. Cut into squares and fold in half or into triangles. Place on a baking sheet and bake for 15 minutes. Dust with confectioners' sugar.

❖ *Yield: 2 dozen*

Index

Almond
  honey fruitcake, 86–87
  zucchini bread, 129
Apple
  bars, 93
  breakfast, loaf, 73
  chewy, loaf, 75
  cooking tip, 73
  crumb muffins, 145–46
  -dumpling muffins, 48–50
  morning glory muffins,
    26–27
  -nut muffins, 51–53
  raisin, coffee cake, 90–91
Applesauce
  loaf, 74
  mincemeat, cake, 171
  squares, 95
Apricots, dried
  honey fruitcake, 86–87

Baking powder
  baking tips, 54–55
  biscuits, 14
baking tips
  baking powder, 54–55
  blueberries, keeping intact
    while baking, 57
  carrot cupcakes, freezing to
    store, 130
  cookie decoration, 190
  cranberries, using frozen, 46

frosting texture, 174
fruitcake, easy removal
  from pan, 86
meringue, readiness, 201
oat bran, successful use of,
  116–17
pastry bag substitute, 70
raspberries, baking with, 67
storage, fruit breads, 82
sugar, cooking/burnt, 148
upside-down cake turning,
  96–97
working with your hands,
  145–46
Banana-nut muffins, 54–55
Biscuits, baking powder, 14
Black bottom cupcakes,
  162–63
Black bottom muffins, 152
Blueberry
  baking tips, 57
  muffins, 56–59
  quick berry pastry squares,
    98–99
  red, white, and blue
    muffins, 68–69
  upside-down squares, 96
Breads, buns, and rolls, yeast
  Bethlehem rolls, 179
  maple walnut coffee cake,
    168–69
  rum spice buns, 209–11

Breads, quick (no yeast)
  applesauce loaf, 74
  breakfast apple loaf, 73
  chewy apple loaf, 75
  cornbread, 13
  cranberry loaf (fruitcake-
    type), 76–77
  crumb spice cake, 165
  currant loaf (fruitcake-
    type), 78–79
  date nut bread, 28–29
  German coffee cake, 166–67
  gingerbread, 158
  molasses loaf, 159
  nut loaf, 30–31
  nut ring, 32
  oatmeal loaf, 124–25
  peanut butter loaf, 33
  pecan loaf, 34
  prune nut loaf, 80
  pumpkin loaf, 126–27
  raisin apple coffee cake,
    90–91
  raisin quick bread, 81
  rhubarb loaf, 128
  Skidmore loaf, 82
  storage tip, fruit breads, 82
  supper loaf, 160
  zucchini bread, 129
Brownies
  German cream cheese,
    194–95

Brownies (*cont.*)
marble walnut, 36–37
mint, 202–3
oat bran, 134
Butter chews, 180
Butterscotch
chews, 181
Congo squares, 187
heavenly layer cookies, 199

Cakes and cupcakes. *See also*
Coffee cakes
black bottom cupcakes,
162–63
blueberry upside-down
squares, 96
butterfly cupcakes, 164
carrot cupcakes, 130–31
cranberry loaf (fruitcake),
76–77
cream cheese holiday cake,
170
cupcakes, my favorite,
172–73
E-Z cupcakes, 161
Hawaiian sponge, 83
holiday fruitcake, 84–85
honey fruitcake, 86–87
low-fat cake, 88
mincemeat applesauce
cake, 171
orange fruitcake, 89
removal of fruitcakes from
pan, tip, 86
upside-down cake turning
tip, 96–97
zucchini chocolate cake,
132
Cake frosting. *See* Icings
Caramel-nut squares, 182

Cardamom, 120
Carrot
cupcakes, 130–31
morning glory muffins,
26–27
muffins, 111–13
Cherry cookies, 100
Chocolate
black bottom cupcakes,
162–63
black bottom muffins, 152
-chip cookies, 183
-chip muffins, 150–51
choco-marshmallow
cookies, 184–85
cookie bars, 188
crisp toffee bars, 189
E-Z cookie bars, 196
fudge icing, 135
fudge squares, 197
German cream cheese
brownies, 194–95
heavenly layer cookies, 199
marble walnut brownies,
36–37
meringue cookies, 201
mint brownies, 202–3
oat bran brownies, 134
rum balls, 206–7
-strawberry muffins, 153
-white chocolate chunk
muffins, 154–55
zucchini chocolate cake,
132
Cobblers, peach, muffins,
62–63
Coconut
butter chews, 180
cookie bars, 188
cookies, 186

E-Z cookie bars, 196
heavenly layer cookies, 199
macaroon drops, 200
piña colada muffins, 64–65
Coffee cake
crumb spice cake, 165
German, 166–67
maple walnut, 168–69
raisin apple, 90–91
sour cream, 175
spice, 176–77
streusel-filled, 178
Confections
butter chews, 180
butterscotch chews, 181
crisp toffee bars, 189
peanut butter fluffs, 204
rum balls, 206–7
Cookies
apple bars, 93
applesauce squares, 95
bars, 188
butter chews, 180
butterscotch chews, 181
caramel-nut squares, 182
cherry, 100
chocolate chip, 183
choco-marshmallow,
184–85
Christmas, 190–91
coconut, 186
Congo squares, 187
cornflake, 133
crisp toffee bars, 189
E-Z, bars, 196
gingerbread, 198
heavenly layer, 199
macaroon drops, 200
meringue, 201
oatmeal drop, 136

peanut butter, 205
sugar, 192–93
Corn
-bread, 13
muffins, 114–15
Cornflake cookies, 133
Cranberry
baking with, tip, 46
cran-orange muffins, 60–61
loaf (fruitcake), 76–77
Cream cheese
black bottom cupcakes,
162–63
black bottom muffins, 152
German, brownies, 194–95
holiday cake, 170
pastries, 212
quick berry pastry squares,
98–99
strawberry-cream muffin,
70–71
Cupcakes. *See* Cakes and
cupcakes
Currant loaf (fruitcake),
78–79

Date
holiday fruitcake, 84–85
nut bread, 28–29
orange fruitcake, 89

Fruitcake
cranberry loaf, 76–77
holiday, 84–85
honey, 86–87
orange, 89
removal from pan, tips, 86
Fudge
icing, 135
squares, 197

Gingerbread, 158
cookies, 198

Honey fruitcake, 86–87

Icings
brown sugar coconut/nut,
125
caramel coconut/nut, 83
chocolate, 184–85
drizzle, 79
fudge, 135
mint, 202–3
my favorite, 174
rum, 209–11

Lemon-poppy seed muffins,
23–25

Macaroon drops, 200
Mace
about, 54
banana nut muffins, 55
Maple walnut coffee cake,
168–69
Meringue cookies, 201
Mincemeat
-applesauce cake, 171
cranberry loaf, 76–77
Mint brownies, 202–3
Molasses loaf, 159
Muffins
apple crumb, 145–46
apple dumpling, 48–50
apple nut, 51–53
banana nut, 54–55
black bottom, 152
blueberry, 56–59
burnt sugar, 148–49
carrot, 111–13

chocolate chip, 150–51
chocolate-strawberry, 153
chocolate-white chocolate
chunk, 154–55
corn, 114–15
glazed orange, 156–57
lemon poppy seed, 23–25
morning glory, 26–27
oat bran, 116–18
peach cobbler, 62–63
piña colada, 64–65
pumpkin, 120–21
raisin bran, 122–23
raspberry, 67
red, white, and blue, 68–69
strawberry-cream, 70–71

Nuts. *See also* Pecan; Walnut
apple nut muffins, 51–53
banana nut muffins, 54
cranberry loaf, 76–77
date nut bread, 28–29
loaf, 30–31
mincemeat applesauce
cake, 171
prune nut loaf, 80
ring, 32
Skidmore loaf, 82

Oat bran
brownies, 134
muffins, 116–18
Oatmeal
drop cookies, 136
fudge squares, 197
loaf, 124–25
Orange
cran-, muffins, 60–61
fruitcake, 89
glazed, muffins, 156–57

Pancake batter, 12
Pastries
  Bethlehem rolls, 179
  butter chews, 180
  butterscotch chews, 181
  caramel-nut squares, 182
  cream cheese, 212
  pecan tarts, 35
  quick berry pastry squares,
    98–99
Peach cobbler muffins,
  62–63
Peanut butter
  cookies, 205
  fluffs, 204
  loaf, 33
  oatmeal drop cookies,
    136
Pecan
  applesauce loaf, 74
  Bethlehem rolls, 179
  caramel-nut squares, 182
  Congo squares, 187
  holiday fruitcake, 84–85
  loaf, 34
  nut loaf, 30–31
  supper loaf, 160
  tarts, 35
Piña colada muffins, 64–65
Pineapple
  Hawaiian sponge cake, 83
  morning glory muffins,
    26–27
  piña colada muffins, 64–65
Poppy seed, lemon-, muffins,
  23–25
Prune
  honey fruitcake, 86–87
  nut loaf, 80

Pumpkin
  loaf, 126–27
  muffins, 120–21

Quick breads. See Breads,
  quick (no-yeast)

Raisin
  -apple coffee cake, 90–91
  bran muffins, 122–23
  honey fruitcake, 86–87
  low-fat cake, 88
  oat bran brownies, 134
  quick bread, 81
  Skidmore loaf, 82
Raspberry
  baking with, tips, 67
  muffins, 67
  quick berry pastry squares,
    98–99
  red, white, and blue
    muffins, 68–69
  store-bought versus home-
    baked, 46–47
Rhubarb loaf, 128
Rum
  balls, 206–7
  spice buns, 209–11

Skidmore loaf, 82
Strawberry
  chocolate-, muffins,
    153
  -cream muffins, 70–71
  quick berry pastry squares,
    98–99
Streusel filling, 178
Streusel topping, 147
Sugar cookie, 192–93

Tarts
  pecan, 35
  quick berry pastry squares,
    98–99

Walnut
  apple nut muffins, 51–53
  applesauce loaf, 74
  butter chews, 180
  Bethlehem rolls, 179
  breakfast apple loaf, 73
  chewy apple loaf, 75
  cream cheese holiday cake,
    170
  crisp toffee bars, 189
  date nut bread, 28–29
  E-Z cookie bars, 196
  heavenly layer cookies, 199
  holiday fruitcake, 84–85
  honey fruitcake, 86–87
  maple walnut coffee cake,
    168–69
  marble, brownies, 36–37
  meringue cookies, 201
  morning glory muffins,
    26–27
  nut ring, 32
  orange fruitcake, 89
  rum balls, 206–7
  streusel filling, 178
  streusel topping, 147
Walnut, black
  nut loaf, 30–31
Wheat, whole bran
  raisin bran muffins, 122–23

Zucchini
  bread, 129
  chocolate cake, 132